DATE DUE

DEMCO 38-296

Benedict Arnold
The Dark Eagle

Benedict Arnold

The Dark Eagle

by

BRIAN RICHARD BOYLAN

W · W · NORTON & COMPANY · INC · *NEW YORK*

Library of Congress Cataloging in Publication Data
Boylan, Brian Richard.
    Benedict Arnold.
    Bibliography: p.
      1. Arnold, Benedict, 1741–1801. 2. André, John,
1751–1780. 3. United States—History—Revolution.
E278.A7B69 1973   973.3'092'4 [B]   73–4235
ISBN 0-393-07471-4

2 3 4 5 6 7 8 9 0

*This book is dedicated to the memory of
Clair Roskam, a dear friend who was one
of the first to encourage this project.*

La ci darem la mano

Contents

Foreword   *11*

Acknowledgments   *19*

Prologue   *25*

PART ONE

1. *The Battle of Saratoga*   *27*
2. *Quebec*   *49*
3. *The Father of the American Navy*   *69*
4. *Arnold's Enemies Gather*   *80*
5. *The Road to Saratoga*   *99*

PART TWO

6. *John André*   *119*
7. *The Captain, the Tory, and the General*   *142*
8. *Arnold Under Attack*   *155*
9. *Arnold Turns*   *163*
10. *Hard Bargaining*   *173*
11. *The Conspiracy Blossoms*   *185*
12. *The Meeting in the Firs*   *196*
13. *André in Flight*   *203*

PART THREE

14. *An Eye for an Eye*   *220*
15. *The Fallen Eagle*   *239*
16. *The Romantic Legend of John André*   *247*

Epilogue   *254*
Bibliography   *258*
Index   *263*

Illustrations

Photographs appear following page 128

Benedict Arnold

Margaret Shippen (Mrs. Benedict Arnold)

Major John André, a self-portrait

Arnold's march to Quebec

"God Blesse Our Armes"—Arnold at Valcour Island

Sir Henry Clinton

General John Burgoyne

West Point as it appeared at the close of the war

Arnold's nameless monument at Saratoga

André's monument in Westminster Abbey

Maps
By Theodore R. Miller

Arnold's and Montgomery's Invasion of Quebec   *51*

Arnold Delays Carleton's Invasion on Lake Champlain   *71*
    INSET: *Naval Battle of Valcour Island*

Burgoyne's Invasion   *105*

Arnold's Decisive Action at the Second Battle of
    Freeman's Farm   *115*

André's Capture and Arnold's Flight   *199*

Foreword

BENEDICT ARNOLD is an enigmatic figure in American history. Until today, he has been comfortably labeled a traitor and a scoundrel, yet historical evidence clearly indicates that he was one of Revolutionary America's greatest heroes.

Arnold is an enigma and a paradox: the greatest of Continental generals and the trusted friend of George Washington, but the man who plotted to betray America to the British.

If one assumes that Arnold was destined to become a traitor, as virtually every American historian has done, then it is a simple matter to dismiss his military achievements as accidents, since no traitor could be a really good American general. Everything he did on behalf of the American cause can be written off as a prelude to his treason.

But it is the purpose of this history to assume that we Americans are sufficiently mature to be able to understand the pressures that drove Benedict Arnold into the arms of the British. Remember, from King Goerge's point of view, a view shared by many Americans loyal to the Crown during the Revolution, men like Arnold were merely returning to their true allegiance. What was treason to one man was patriotism and loyalty to his neighbor.

The American Revolution was like no other war in modern history in that Americans were divided in their allegiances and there was much shifting of positions throughout the war. At the outbreak of the Revolution, the majority of American colonists considered a total rupture with the Mother Country unthinkable. Total independence was an idea of a few fanatics. There were many families who quietly coasted through the Revolution, seeming to espouse the cause of whichever faction happened to be in power or in possession of their city, waiting for the ultimate outcome of the war.

Nowhere is this ambivalence more sharply underlined than in the higher reaches of society. There are numerous accounts of balls and parties in which professed Tories rubbed elbows amicably with out-and-out rebels. In cities like Boston, New York, Philadelphia, and Newport—where the rebel command of today might be replaced by the British garrison tomorrow—social circles had to remain fluid in order to accommodate the officers and partisans of both sides.

At the outbreak of hostilities, America's spokesman at the foreign courts was Benjamin Franklin, who remained steadfast in his adherence to the principles of independence. His illegitimate son, William, however, was the Royal Governor of New Jersey and stayed with the Tories throughout the war. The military leaders on both sides had fought together on the British side against the French fifteen years earlier. George Washington and Beverley Robinson were old friends but became official enemies. Generals Horatio Gates, Philip Schuyler and Charles Lee had fought with the British but donned American uniforms. And Sir Henry Clinton, commander in chief of the British troops, grew up in America as the son of the Royal Governor of New York.

Benedict Arnold was not a simple black-and-white, good-and-evil man, but rather a complex, complicated individual who did what he did out of deep conviction and personal feeling.

Like most Americans, I first heard about Benedict Arnold in school as a scoundrel whose name was synonymous with treason. Yet when several years ago I began to study the Benedict Arnold–John André conspiracy, I wondered about the one-sided portraits of Arnold. Fortunately, I discovered two authors, John Hyde Preston (*Revolution:1776—A Short History of the American Revolution*) and Kenneth Roberts (*Arundel* and *Rabble in Arms*), who treated Arnold sympathetically. Preston was the historian and Roberts the novelist, yet both dwelt on Arnold's personal magnetism and his shabby treatment by the government.

With these books as refutations of the popular Arnold-as-scoundrel theory, I moved east from Chicago in 1964 and started a period of intensive research that was to extend over many years—and has yet to end. I was determined to discover whether Benedict Arnold was a great general and/or a vile traitor—or was perhaps somewhere between these extremes—and I was also intrigued by the story of his conspiracy which involved the tragic young British officer, Major André.

To supplement my readings in libraries and historical archives, I set out to travel and photograph the routes of Arnold and André in their various phases of involvement in the Revolution and the great conspiracy which nearly destroyed American independence.

On the way, I have discovered many strange and fascinating facts and characters, some of them well known in history, other known only to specialists on the American Revolution.

Yet at almost every stage of my research I ran head-long into the enigma of Benedict Arnold. Who was the real Benedict Arnold—the man who marched through the blizzards of Maine to attack British-held Quebec or the man who sent the British top-secret information in order to enable them to capture General Washington? The man who, stripped of command, recklessly led the American troops to victory at Saratoga or the man who turned down Washington's offer of the number-two field command in the Continental army? The man who built a fleet and held the mighty British navy at bay on Lake Champlain or the British officer who presided over the burning of New London? The American general who routed the British and Indians in the Mohawk Valley by the simple ruse of a rumor or the secret conspirator who ran to the British with his tail between his legs when the conspiracy was detected?

Because of his enigma—the greatness and tragedy of one man—Benedict Arnold is the most fascinating partici-pant in the American Revolution. He was neither all virtue nor all evil. He was compassionate toward his enemies, yet after his defection almost savage toward his former friends and colleagues. The man who could inspire a shrunken army of starving, frozen, barefoot soldiers to keep on marching until they reached Quebec could not attract more than a handful of followers to the British cause when he changed sides.

Benedict Arnold was the most notorious traitor of the Revolution, yet his treason helped to solidify the Americans against the British. Like many brilliant leaders, Arnold had as many enemies and persecutors as he had friends and supporters.

While he was a rebel general, Arnold's strongest supporters were George Washington and his fellow generals, yet after his defection to the British, Washington and his colleagues yearned vengefully to capture and hang their former friend./A key figure in the American rebellion against Britain, Arnold was most comfortable in the company of the conservatives who were less than enthusiastic about the idea of independence.

Arnold is not an easy historical figure to study objectively. The British historians have paid little attention to him, while even the most sympathetic American biographers seem compelled to damn him loudly and at length despite his accomplishments.

Rather than clutter the text with footnotes, I have chosen to lump the sources and bibliography at the end of the book. Wherever possible original manuscripts and texts have been consulted. Dubious quotes and hoary myths (such as the one describing Arnold asking for his American uniform on his deathbed) have been discarded. An occasional legend has been included, and clearly labeled, only if it has the ring of truth to it.

What I have tried to impart in the following pages is the sense of immediacy and present touch with past events which cannot but affect anyone who travels across Arnold country. I've stood on the few stones that remain of the ferry dock on the west bank of the Hudson where Arnold paced back and forth waiting to meet with Major André, who was on the other side of the river. I've stood atop Teller's Point, where a groggy but furious Colonel Livingston rubbed his hands in the chilly autumn dawn and gave orders to his gunners to shell the British sloop of war anchored impudently a few hundred yards away from the American lines.

I've driven and walked along Major André's escape route and examined the monument on the site of his capture, a monument to the three bandits who just happened to save the American Revolution by their desire for gold. I have sat at Major André's desk in the Jumel Mansion in New York, and I have paced the tiny room where he was imprisoned in Tappan, New York. I have walked the long route that Major John André, adjutant general of the British army, marched to his execution.

I have explored the paths of West Point, hearing the rapid, restless tapping of Benedict Arnold's cane as he inspected the fortress he was preparing to hand over to the British. I've stood in the halls and rooms of the Ford Mansion in Morristown, where an embittered Benedict Arnold pleaded with Washington first to give him an exciting command position and then, after he had sold himself to the British, to be appointed commander of West Point.

And perhaps the most exciting experience for me was to walk along the path used by Benedict Arnold when he led his men into the British fortification at Saratoga, clinching the American victory and bringing about the French alliance that helped win the war.

In any of these places, particularly the Saratoga battlefield on an October day, one can almost see and hear the impetuous Arnold, sword in hand, cape flying, galloping across the battlefield, hoarsely urging his "brave lads" on, defying the British cannon and muskets—certain death—to achieve a stunning victory.

The romantic, heroic Benedict Arnold has been lost in the vilification of the traitor, and I have attempted to restore this as a balance to the unpleasantness we all learned about the man in school.

He was no saint, but then he was no devil either.

BRIAN RICHARD BOYLAN

November 1972

Acknowledgments

My FIRST TASTE OF the American Revolution arrived at 10:00 A.M. on the first day of school in mid-September, 1951, in the person of Michael Ganey. A giant of a man—a former tackle at Notre Dame and now a teacher of American history to sophomores at Loyola Academy in Chicago —he stormed into the room, banged his books down on his desk, and undertook the task of shaking from our minds all the misconceptions and fables about American history which we had been accumulating throughout elementary school, from our parents, and from our environments.

It was Michael Ganey who first heaved a rock at the alabaster sainthood of George Washington as sculpted by the Reverend Jared Sparks. We learned that Washington was very much a man, a man with a foul temper which he had to keep constantly in check, a man who could curse with gusto, and a man who enjoyed both wine and women.

This remarkable teacher loosened his students up with irreverent references to "Gentleman Johnny" Burgoyne, then he shocked them with the news that Benedict Arnold was more than just a traitor, that he was one of America's finest generals.

Mike Ganey struck a spark in at least one of his students that would eventually grow to a bonfire in several years, and for that spark he deserves the first credit in this book. His tragic death in an accident a few years after he taught me causes me regret that this one outstanding history teacher cannot read these fruits of his teaching.

Another man who deserves acknowledgment, and who is very much alive, is Wayne M. Daniels, who, as well as being a good friend, has been a bottomless well of information about colonial America and the Revolution in particular. Together we have sought out the sites of the Arnold-André conspiracy as we collaborated on a screenplay about André's role in it. We have exchanged photographs and slides, and side by side pored through original documents in the Rare Book Room of the New York Public Library. It was Wayne who copied out the log of H.M.S. *Vulture* for those eventful days. Whenever I have been stumped for detail that might add a bit of color to the narrative, Wayne was always there with the answer, or else a suggestion as to where that answer could be found.

It is customary to acknowledge the help of chief librarians in the many major research centers, but since most of my research had been completed before I even thought about a book, I did not deal with the top echelons, so I can only extend my thanks to the many nameless sublibrarians who assisted me. However, I must extend deepest thanks to Mrs. June Adams and her staff at the Westwood, New Jersey Public Library for their helpfulness in tracking down sources, obtaining inter-library loans, and letting me hold on to valuable reference books throughout the writing of this manuscript.

Once into the manuscript, I received invaluable guidance and suggestion from my editor, Starling Lawrence. His enthusiasm kept me going through the long grind of turning out a final manuscript.

Nicholas H. MacMichael, Keeper of the Muniments at Westminster Abbey, was especially helpful in supplying information about Major André's reinterment at the Abbey.

Also, I must thank the many nameless historians and students with the National Park Service, as well as those involved with state or locally maintained historic sites and buildings. Each historian has his own favorites among the parks and historic sites, and if pushed to name my favorite, I choose the Saratoga National Battlefield as the best-restored and best-preserved.

My final thanks must go to the actors, producers, playwrights, and technical crews who are so much a part of my other life as a theatrical director. Their patience and good will enabled me to turn from Poe and Cervantes to Arnold and André.

Benedict Arnold
The Dark Eagle

The Dark Eagle comes to claim the Wilderness. The Wilderness will yield to the Dark Eagle, but the Rock will defy him. The Dark Eagle will soar aloft to the Sun. Nations will behold him and sound his praises. Yet when he soars highest his fall is most certain. When his wings brush the sky then the arrow will pierce his heart.

—Greeting attributed to Natanis when he first met Arnold in 1775

Prologue

ON THE BATTLEFIELD of Saratoga, atop a gentle slope where the guns of the British Breymann redoubt defied the American forces, stands an unnamed monument. The front of the monument depicts a military boot, and the back of the monument is inscribed:

In memory of the most brilliant soldier in the Continental Army, who was desperately wounded on this spot, the sally port, Burgoyne's Great Western Redubt, 7th October, 1777, winning for his countrymen the decisive battle of the American Revolution and for himself the rank of Major General.

"The most brilliant soldier in the Continental army"?

George Washington? Anthony Wayne? Nathanael Greene? Daniel Morgan?

No, the monument is dedicated to the man whom Washington so trusted as to offer him command of the left wing, the number-two position in the Continental army; a man who, time and again, defeated or delayed the British with his daring strategy.

Why, then, is he not named and properly honored? Because the "most brilliant soldier in the Continental army," and the man whose victory at Saratoga brought France into the American fight against the British, is a man whose name cannot be mentioned with respect in any American classroom or by any political orator. His name is Benedict Arnold.

PART ONE

1. The Battle of Saratoga

THE BATTLE of Saratoga was to have been a conventional, European-style combat, with both sides marching, counter-marching, driving in pickets, attacking exposed flanks with cavalry until a brief, final battle would shatter the enemy's lines, forcing an immediate surrender. That is the way Major General Horatio Gates, commander of the Army of the North, wanted it. Gates, a former British soldier, now was at his summit as the commanding general of the Continental army, which was drawn up along the western shores of the Hudson River to await the once indomitable British army on October 7, 1777.

Gates had planned everything to perfection. The British, under command of the playwright-playboy General John ("Gentleman Johnny") Burgoyne, had been worn down by a long march from Canada, while the Continental forces had been daily augmented by fresh militia volunteers who responded to calls throughout the colonies to rout the British invaders.

In order to reach Albany, New York, and then march south with supporting British troops and cut the colonies in two, Burgoyne had crossed to the west bank of the Hudson and was moving rapidly toward Albany. But

Gates had foreseen this move and had selected the hilly eminence of Bemis Heights near the village of Stillwater. Bemis Heights commanded the only road along the river leading to Albany, and for Burgoyne to pass the American fortifications, he would have to divert his army from its hasty march—October in the north country means that snow and winter are coming soon—and force a battle with the rebels. Burgoyne had cut his supply line when he crossed the Hudson, and he had to forge on with only a few days' food and equipment for his dwindling army of British regulars and Hessian and Brunswick mercenaries. If he could only reach Albany, Burgoyne could settle in for the winter and then, the following spring, join with a British force from New York City to cleave the colonies.

Gates knew what Burgoyne was thinking, and he carefully deployed the American defenses along the west bank of the Hudson to lure the British into a trap from which they could not escape. Horatio Gates was a traditional soldier who believed that outmaneuvering an enemy was far more satisfactory and predictable than engaging in open combat. A trapped enemy had to surrender, whereas an enemy confronted with a life-or-death battle could well rally and possibly defeat the defending Continental forces —many of whom were untrained militia.

And just as Gates's plans were coming to fruition, following an indecisive open-field battle at Freeman's Farm a few weeks earlier, a cloud of dust on his left dashed his well-planned victory into a potential disaster.

The cloud of dust was from the galloping white mare of the one man who could upset Gates's plans, the officer whom Gates had carefully stripped of command and ordered to remain in his quarters on that day of the ultimate battle. And the horse was carrying the man at breakneck speed toward the battle front.

Like many modern generals, Gates had stationed himself well beyond the field of battle, relying on his couriers to bring him accounts of what was happening and to relay his orders to the field generals. Standing outside the red clapboard house that served as his headquarters, Gates could hear the roar of cannon and musketry in the distance, and clouds of smoke billowed on the horizon.

Watching in fury as the white mare carried its rider toward combat, Gates turned and savagely commanded an aide to order the officer to return to his quarters at once.

But no horse was fast enough to overtake Benedict Arnold that day. Catching up with stray regiments and stragglers, he ordered them to follow him into action. When the soldiers saw General Benedict Arnold shouting to them, they turned immediately and ran after the fiery officer whose exploits during the American Revolution had filled friend as well as enemy with fear and respect for his military prowess. As he galloped toward the sound of the cannon, Benedict Arnold carried with him a reputation as a scrapper, a man who could not be outgeneraled, one who inevitably turned defeat into victory. His friends loved him and would follow him into the blaze of British muskets; his enemies hated him, yet admired his courage.

Since the earlier battle of Freeman's Farm, which was a draw, the British had thrown up a series of redoubts—log-and-mud barricades—to protect them from attack and to use as rallying points. By the time Benedict Arnold and his hastily gathered forces arrived at the scene of combat, the British were firing from behind these redoubts, and every American attempt to storm them had failed. The

Americans were forced to fight in the open, which suited the well-trained British. During the earlier encounter at Freeman's Farm, the Americans had been able to fall back into the woods and practice their inimitable brand of guerrilla warfare which so terrorized the British, who did not know where to fire or how to combat an unseen enemy. But once the Americans had to come out into the open fields, the British had the advantage.

It is difficult for generations raised since the Civil War to realize the importance of the bayonet in military charges during the Revolution. The musket was so clumsy in its loading and inaccurate in its firing power that it could only be discharged once, at the beginning of an attack that would be carried out chiefly by bayonets and musket butts. Musket fire was only accidentally deadly, but what struck fear into the hearts of militiamen was the sight of a line of bayonets advancing swiftly upon them.

For the attackers, the first discharge of muskets was mainly to make noise and create a smoke screen through which to attack. For the defenders, they had one musket load with which to fire, then it was bayonet against bayonet.

Of course, cannon played a heavy part in an attack, and if the artillery chiefs were at all competent, they could bombard the enemy with deadly fusillades of cannon ball, exploding shells, and grapeshot.

True, rifles were used during the Revolution, most notably by Dan Morgan's Virginians, but these were still muzzle-loading weapons, and the ball had to be small enough to be forced down the rifle muzzle yet capable of expanding from the explosion of powder behind it to revolve through the rifle grooves.

Arnold saw immediately that the only way to defeat the British would be a reckless storming of the two main redoubts, located several hundred yards apart. Directly in front of his troops was the formidable Balcarres redoubt— named for the British general, the Earl of Balcarres. To the north was the Breymann redoubt—named for the Brunswick general whose forces were deployed around this makeshift fortress. The Breymann redoubt was on a slight elevation and its guns could offer some protection to the Balcarres redoubt forces. However, both redoubts were the scene of active fighting, and Arnold quickly ordered the four regiments he had gathered to charge the enemy troops in front of the Balcarres redoubt.

Unlike Gates, who preferred to command from behind the lines, Arnold always led from in front of his troops, and this charge was no exception.

Arnold led charge after charge against the Balcarres redoubt, forcing the British and mercenary troops to take refuge behind the log barricades, but it seemed impossible to penetrate the defenses. Arnold was regrouping his forces when he heard the sounds of battle to his left, in the vicinity of the Breymann redoubt. Urging his troops to try one more offensive against the Balcarres redoubt, Benedict Arnold spurred his horse to the north, cutting directly across the field of fire and miraculously escaping death from British bullets. If the Balcarres redoubt was difficult to take, then perhaps the Breymann redoubt would be easier.

Arnold arrived to take command of a disarrayed force of two regiments and Daniel Morgan's crack Virginia riflemen, who had been unable to storm the Breymann redoubt. Knowing that the traditional British redoubt always had a rear opening known as the sally port, Arnold directed several of his men to concentrate a heavy fire on the front of the redoubt while he led a band of men in a circular movement around to the rear.

Breymann's forces were completely surrounded now, and Arnold intended to capture the redoubt personally. Charging up a small rise, which today is covered with tall grass and wild flowers, Arnold signaled with his sword for the final assault. Just as he entered the redoubt, his horse was shot from under him and another bullet crashed into his left thighbone, the same leg that had been wounded during the siege of Quebec.

As Arnold went down, his men surged into the make-shift fortress with bayonets and muskets swinging, until the enemy forces surrendered. Arnold's men found the soldier who had wounded their general, a German mer-cenary. "Don't hurt him, boys!" Arnold cried, despite his pain. "He's a fine fellow. He only did his duty."

This was Benedict Arnold at his finest. Wounded for the second time in the same leg, he was still concerned lest his assailant be mistreated for doing his duty.

As Arnold lay in pain, his troops were capturing the Breymann redoubt and thus ensuring the American victory at Saratoga. General Gates's messenger, who had finally caught up with Arnold, realized that it would be academic to order the stricken general back to his tent. Already, a litter was being prepared to carry Arnold back to the American lines. Gates's messenger knew that Arnold had achieved precisely what Gates had been afraid of—a battle-field victory. Gates's strategy was washed away by the heroic exploits of this foolhardy field general.

Henry Dearborn, who had marched with Arnold

through the frozen Maine wilderness for the assault on Quebec, wrote that as soon as he saw Arnold wounded, he rushed to his side.

"Where are you hit?" he asked.

"In the same leg. I wish it had been my heart," Arnold replied. This was Arnold's final moment of glory. Ten days after this victory, General Burgoyne surrendered his army —not to Arnold but to Horatio Gates—in Saratoga. Gates got his revenge on Arnold by barely mentioning him in his reports to Congress and to Washington. But Arnold's colleagues saw to it that Congress and the commander in chief were properly informed about Arnold's heroism, through letters and by word of mouth.

Saratoga was Benedict Arnold's one significant victory, yet he was highly regarded by his fellow officers as well as feared by his British opponents. The man had a mercurial quality, a reckless bravado which constantly inspired troops to rally from certain defeat to fight again. Even when he lost battles, he made sure that the British suffered mightily. And his troops loved him. Arnold is certainly the only American general—at a time when the American cause seemed lost—who could have rallied the forces at Saratoga by his daring ride in the face of enemy fire. During his march on Quebec the previous year, when half his command had turned back or fallen in the snow, Arnold continued to lead his men on with a cheerfulness and determination that wrung the last drop of perseverance from them.

Sir John Fortescue, a British military historian, has captured the essence of Arnold in one paragraph.

In natural military genius neither Washington nor Greene are to my mind comparable with Benedict Arnold. The man . . . possessed all the gifts of a great commander. To boundless energy and enterprise he united quick insight into a situation, sound strategic instinct, audacity of movement, wealth of resource, a swift and unerring eye in action, great personal daring and true magic of leadership. It was he and no other who beat Burgoyne at Saratoga and, with Daniel Morgan to command the militia, Benedict Arnold was the most formidable opponent that could be matched against the British in America.

Who was this man who ranked even higher than Washington in the estimation of his enemies and military historians? A onetime apothecary and bookseller who became a successful merchant, Benedict Arnold spent his early years in pre-Revolutionary Connecticut.

Born on January 14, 1741, in Norwich, Benedict was one of six children—all but two of whom died at an early age—of a once prosperous merchant and ship captain and his wife. Although Arnold's father was widely respected in Norwich, the decline and failure of his business ventures caused him to seek relief in liquor, a situation which grew increasingly worse as the years passed. In order to keep the impetuous young Benedict out of trouble, his mother apprenticed him to her cousins, Daniel and Joseph Lathrop, who ran a prosperous apothecary shop in Norwich.

Young Benedict was growing up in the heady atmosphere of the French and Indian War (known in Europe as the Seven Years' War because it was fought from 1756 to 1763). The war was to shatter French power in North America and establish Britain's supremacy—and power—in the American colonies and Canada.

Regularly, recruiting squads would march through the streets of Norwich, drums rattling and fifes screeching. The call would be made for volunteers, and Arnold was ready to leave at once. His mother and the Lathrops, however, were not agreeable, and Benedict resumed his chores in the store.

Historians are vague about exactly when Benedict Arnold got his first taste of military life. One of the reasons for this vagueness is that contemporaries of the young Arnold told so many patriotic lies about him after he joined the British that it is difficult to determine precise dates. (One example of the mob's fury at Arnold was its destruction of the gravestones of Arnold's dead brothers and sisters and parents.)

Arnold's mother died on August 15, 1759, and sometime thereafter Arnold joined a company of militia for a very brief time and saw no action. Two years later, his father, who by then had become a public drunk, also died. Arnold and his only surviving sister, Hannah, decided to leave Norwich for the larger, more challenging port of New Haven. During recent years, Arnold had been actively engaged in the trading end of the Lathrop business, which involved sailing to the other New England ports, the West Indies, and even London. On these trips he learned how to bargain and how to buy drugs, merchandise, and books.

But there is nothing unusual in such a biographical note, and it offers us little insight into the mind and character of the young Benedict Arnold. Again, we have only the sketchiest reliable evidence about his boyhood, but all accounts agree that he was always filled with a tremendous store of nervous energy. Also, since he stood five feet seven inches high, he seemed determined to show the world that shortness was no criterion for judging a man's worth. Although not tall, the young Arnold developed his body to physical perfection, delighting in acrobatics, tumbling, and various other stunts to prove his physical prowess. His shoulders were broad and his chest big. As an adolescent, he seems to have expended considerable energy in typical pranks and mischief. One aspect of Arnold is certain, and that is his famous temper. All his contemporaries refer to it, and we shall have opportunity to see it at work in later years.

Arnold quickly established himself in New Haven in a shop beneath a shingle reading:

B. ARNOLD
Druggist, Bookseller, &c.
From London
Sibi Totique

It was fashionable to add a motto after one's name, and the Latin one Arnold had chosen means "for himself and for all." In the shop, Arnold had stocked the shelves with elixirs, powders, balms, spices, herbs, watches and jewelry, prints, stationery, sugar, tea, and books. In fact, Arnold's shop was in many ways prophetic of the evolution of the modern drugstore.

One advantage for the proprietor, however, was that Arnold's restlessness led him to pour his profits from the shop into small ships and sail off each spring up and down the American coast with a cargo of horses and lumber, selling, trading, and buying. In the autumn he returned with cargoes of European goods, sugar, molasses, and rum. In Canada he sold woolen goods and food, and purchased the horses which he would sell in the West Indies and in American ports the following spring.

It was around this busy time of his young career that Arnold ran headlong against one of the realities of business life: creditors had to be paid. During one of his first trips to London as an independent merchant, Arnold carried with him letters of recommendation from the Lathrop brothers. These letters, while politely worded, were vouchers for Arnold's reliability and integrity. But Arnold seemed to be more enthusiastic about the dickering and trading of his seagoing ventures than about keeping accurate account books—a trait that would haunt him throughout his career as an American officer. It was not that Arnold was dishonest or eager to swindle his creditors. Rather, he had more important things to do than to sit down and sort out and settle his debts. When creditors pursued him, as six London firms did in 1768, claiming that he owed them £1,766, Arnold paid them slowly.

Two other incidents give us some view of the pre-war Arnold. One was his marriage and the other his emergence as a political radical. In 1767, Arnold married Margaret ("Peggy") Mansfield, a member of one of New Haven's established merchant families. Although she rapidly bore Arnold three sons, Benedict, Richard, and Henry, Peggy appears not to have matched Arnold's impetuous ardor and, one winter, refused to let him into her bed because of a report she had received that he had contracted venereal disease in the West Indies.

There is little else we know about Peggy Arnold's coolness toward her husband, except his complaints of not receiving any word from her during the long months he spent away from home.

Three years before Arnold's marriage, the British government enacted the Sugar Act, followed by the infamous Stamp Act. The purpose of these and other revenue-producing taxes was to make the American colonies foot all of the bill for Britain's seven-year battle against the French. The various acts passed by Parliament prohibited

American traders from selling or buying their goods any-
where but in England and her colonies. If they did, then
they would have to pay a tax.

Customs inspectors and tariff officials were dispatched
to the colonies to enforce these edicts. By this time,
Benedict Arnold was rapidly moving toward a political
conservatism that would remain with him for the rest of
his life. He believed in free enterprise and was not about
to let some London ignoramuses cheat him out of his right-
ful profit. Like the wealthy Boston merchant John Hancock, Arnold became a smuggler. Although smuggling was
quite common during this period it was fraught with peril
should royal officials catch the smuggler. His goods, ship,
and financial assets were all endangered.

Thus, Arnold was thrown into the ranks of the radicals,
those who opposed the British government's acts. Many
were the stormy meetings held in the New Haven taverns,
with Benedict Arnold's voice louder than the rest in con-
demnation of the customs laws.

During 1766, Arnold's ship, *Fortune*, was threatened
with confiscation when one of his sailors, Peter Boles, tried
to blackmail Arnold into paying him extravagant wages in
return for Boles's not tattling to the customs officials. It
seems that Boles went so far as to seek out the customs
inspector but could not find him—which was fortunate
for Arnold and unfortunate for Boles.

Arnold was furious when he learned this, and he immediately accosted Boles and wrung from him a written
confession and a promise not to inform on anybody in
New England and to leave New Haven at once. When
Boles defied Arnold by remaining in town, Arnold rounded
up a gang of his sailors. "I then made one of the party that

took him to the whipping post, where he received nearly forty lashes with a small cord, and was conducted out of town."

The New Haven elders were shocked at Arnold's behavior, and the grand jury promptly indicted Arnold and his colleagues. Two of the grand jurors were burned in effigy, and large torchlight demonstrations were held on Arnold's behalf. Arnold was found guilty, but the court, heeding the mood of the mob, awarded Boles damages of only fifty shillings.

Arnold's behavior in this instance is not pretty, but it was in keeping with the rising pitch of hatred toward England and her representatives throughout New England. Smugglers bathed their defiance of the King's agents in patriotism, and when the Crown replied with more repressive measures, the smugglers became local heroes. Meanwhile, bands of local hoodlums calling themselves "Sons of Liberty" tormented the King's representatives and eminent Tories by looting and burning their houses, killing their animals, and tarring and feathering them.

Arnold's enthusiasm for the patriot cause was such that when a local militia was formed with the formidable name of the Governor's Fort Guards, Arnold was invited to join and soon was elected captain. He outfitted himself with a coat of scarlet and buff, and white breeches and stockings, and drilled his sixty colleagues on the New Haven green.

When news of the British march on Lexington and Concord and the American resistance reached New Haven, Arnold and his men went wild and prepared to march immediately. But the more conservative New Haven citizens voted for neutrality at a town meeting and appointed a committee to see that peace prevailed in New Haven. But

Arnold and his militia were having none of such talk, and the thirty-four-year-old captain bullied the committee until it released to him the keys to the powder house.

Benedict Arnold first won widespread notice in 1775, when he persuaded the Massachusetts Committee of Public Safety to appoint him to raise an expedition against the British-held stronghold of Fort Ticonderoga. To capture this fort, Arnold reasoned, would be to capture some eighty pieces of heavy cannon, twenty brass cannon, as many as twelve large mortars, and ample arms and munitions— enough for the American forces surrounding Boston to drive out the British invaders.

On May 3, 1775, the committee appointed him to the rank of colonel, with orders to take Ticonderoga, a star-shaped fort at the bottom of Lake Champlain. Since Lake Champlain and the Hudson River constituted the main waterway connection between Canada and the colonies, the commanding position of Lake Champlain was essential for control of this connection. At the outbreak of hostilities between the rebels and the British, Fort Ticonderoga was in tattered condition—having been built many years earlier by the French but subsequently captured by the British— and it was undermanned.

As Arnold set off in his sparkling red coat and white breeches—which would later cause some confusion when redcoats were firing against redcoats—a counterdrama was being enacted in the Catamount Tavern in Bennington, then part of the New Hampshire Grants, a territory which included the entire state of Vermont.

Under the command of a gigantic woodsman, Ethan Allen, an illegal army was organized in the territory that later became Vermont. The Green Mountain Boys made certain that no New York officials (New York State claimed jurisdiction over part of Vermont) made their way into the foothills and mountains that make up much of Vermont. Ethan Allen heard that Massachusetts had sent an officer to raise troops to capture Ticonderoga, and Allen was determined to be in on the action.

After the Boys democratically chose Allen as their commander, they proceeded to do what they usually did in the Catamount Tavern; they got drunk. Some time after Allen had left to plan the campaign against Ticonderoga, the boisterous Boys were astounded to see a dapper officer wearing the colors of Massachusetts and bearing a commission from the Committee of Public Safety with authority to take command of an expedition against Fort Ticonderoga.

The Vermonters were furious and threatened to return home if this upstart superseded Ethan Allen. During the yelling and brawling, Arnold and some of Allen's lieutenants slipped out of the Catamount to find Allen and negotiate with him. Several hours later, the Boys discovered Arnold's departure, no doubt with throbbing hangovers, considering the potency of colonial rum. When they finally overtook Arnold and Allen, the Vermonter placated his Boys by telling them that he and Arnold would share the command, a compromise which they accepted.

They set out at once, the attacking force by now numbering around 250 men, most of them sober and all excited over the prospect of capturing the fort. Although they arrived on the Vermont shore opposite Ticonderoga during the night, they could not cross the lake until just before daybreak, because no one had bothered to arrange for boats to cross the mile-wide stretch of water.

Creeping silently around the imposing walls of the fort, Arnold and Allen and their men discovered to their delight that the gate to the fortress was open and the sentry on duty was snoozing over his musket. The sudden yells of the Boys awoke the sentry, who tried to fire, then fled. A second sentry was captured by Allen, who demanded of him where the commanding officer of the fort was quartered.

Awakened by the shouting and whooping, Lieutenant Jocelyn Feltham leaped out of bed, pulled on a shirt, grabbed his breeches, and threw open the door, only to be confronted by the towering Allen and the nattily uniformed Arnold. Feltham attempted to stall for time, hoping that his own men were aiming their muskets at the loud, ungodly rabble swarming in the courtyard. The lieutenant haughtily asked the two leaders by what authority they had stormed the fort. Allen's reply has become legendary:

"In the name of the Great Jehovah and the Continental Congress!"

The lieutenant might have challenged this reasoning on theological as well as political grounds (since, until that time, neither Allen nor Arnold claimed to have received any divine commissions, and the Continental Congress hadn't the foggiest idea of what was going on. If it had, its members would probably have voted down the attack as provocative).

However, the lieutenant's speculations were interrupted by the garrison's commander, Captain William Delaplace, who, when told that the Green Mountain Boys had effectively disarmed all the soldiers in the garrison, surrendered in the traditional fashion of extending his sword hilt. Which of the two rival leaders accepted it is not known, but it's safe to assume that two hands darted out simultaneously and that Allen, much larger than Arnold, probably had a longer reach.

From that point on, victory was sweet for the Boys, who proceeded to get boisterously drunk on the large quantities of rum they found in the fort. For Arnold and Allen, however, victory was bitter. As the Boys ransacked the fort, stealing whatever was not nailed down, Arnold protested strongly and quoted military law forbidding such practices to the looters, most of whom ignored him or replied by spitting at his feet. At one point, Arnold stopped one of the Boys who was making off with a particularly precious bit of loot, with the victim pleading desperately to get it back. Arnold snatched the prize and returned it to its owner. A moment later the enraged soldier returned, this time with a loaded musket, which he placed directly against Arnold's chest, and demanded that the uniformed colonel acknowledge Ethan Allen's leadership. Arnold replied that he was acting as the official leader appointed by the state of Massachusetts, and that as far as he was concerned, the Green Mountain Boys were a pack of outlaws on a merry spree. Looking straight at his opponent, Arnold stared him down, and the man suddenly lowered the gun and lurched back into combat with the rum.

It took four days for the troops recruited by Arnold and his aides to arm themselves and march to Ticonderoga, and their arrival did much to restore order in the fort. Arnold's men had commandeered a schooner, and Arnold, who had had extensive experience sailing along the Atlantic coast from Connecticut to the Caribbean and up to Newfoundland, rapidly loaded the schooner with some of the captured artillery and set sail for the north to capture the armed British ship reported to be around the northern end of Lake Champlain. When his schooner could go no farther because of a lack of wind, Arnold loaded his forces, thirty-five men, into two rowboats and rowed some thirty miles up the Richelieu River to St. John's, in Canada. Just after dawn, his men swarmed onto the deck of a seventy-ton sloop and captured the entire crew. The prisoners told Arnold that they were expecting a large column of British forces shortly, so Arnold hauled anchor and sailed the sloop down into the wide lake.

Sailing down Lake Champlain with his captured sloop, Benedict Arnold paced the deck in an excellent mood. It was around this time that the men who served under him began to be infected by the man's total personality. Were he running for public office today, he would be described as a man with charisma. The public Arnold was an exciting, stimulating man. At thirty-four years of age, he was in his prime, finally happy in his work. Since there is only one reliable portrait of Benedict Arnold, we are forced to believe the descriptions of his colleagues. He had dark hair (which he later powdered white), his complexion was swarthy, and there was not an ounce of fat on him. He had become a superb horseman and an expert sailor, not to mention fencer and sharpshooter—talents which he was able to put to good use during the Revolution.

But as his men watched their colonel pace the deck with the self-assurance of a seasoned sea dog, they probably saw him suddenly burst into laughter. Rushing to the sides, they saw in the distance several bateaux (flat-bottomed scows, up to 60 feet long) bearing Ethan Allen and a number of his Green Mountain Boys. Determined not to let Arnold grab off any glory on his own, Allen drove his men to row day and night until they came abreast of Arnold's captured ship. Arnold saluted them with a blast of King George's artillery. Allen's men answered with scattered shots from muskets and pistols.

Gracious now that he was the undisputed conqueror, Arnold leaned over the rail and informed the Boys that there was a large supply of rum on board and that they were welcome to it. Within minutes, past grievances were forgotten as Allen's and Arnold's men toasted one another. Allen told him that he had decided to attack St. John's, but when Arnold replied that it had already been done, Allen grumbled that he might as well continue and battle any British troops who might have arrived since Arnold's departure. Arnold loaded Allen with provisions; Allen was not the brightest tactician, and on more than one occasion he set out with his men but forgot to bring along food.

Arnold docked at Crown Point, a fortress a few miles north of Ticonderoga which Arnold's men—volunteers recruited in Massachusetts—had captured before showing up at Ticonderoga. Arnold wrote triumphantly to the Massachusetts Committee of Public Safety and to Congress that he held both Crown Point and Ticonderoga and would continue to do so until Continental forces arrived to haul away the valuable cannon and munitions he had captured. Meanwhile, Allen was proposing an immediate attack on Canada, specifically Montreal and Quebec.

Arnold and Allen were soldiers and impetuous, and had little understanding of the mood of the Continental Congress. The lawyers and politicians in the Continental Congress were continually preaching reconciliation with the mother country. Were it not for firebrands like Samuel

Adams and John Adams, and intellectuals such as Thomas Jefferson and Benjamin Franklin, America might today be paying taxes to Queen Elizabeth II.

On learning of the capture of Ticonderoga, Congress immediately resolved that Arnold and Allen should abandon the fortress and remove all artillery to the south end of Lake George, where it then would be inventoried, "in order that they may be safely returned when the restoration of the former harmony between Great Britain and these colonies so ardently wished for by the latter shall render it prudent."

This congressional fiat met with such an uproar in New England and New York—the hotbeds of anti-British feeling—that the politicians retracted it and agreed to reinforce Ticonderoga and Crown Point.

Although Arnold continued to beseech Congress to let him have enough men and arms to invade and capture Canada, his only answer was an insult from the Massachusetts Committee of Public Safety, which decided to turn over jurisdiction of Crown Point and Ticonderoga to a Connecticut colonel, Benjamin Hinman. Arnold at first ignored this slight, then, when it became official, immediately submitted his resignation. He also demanded of the Massachusetts legislature compensation for the hundreds of pounds which he had paid from his own money, but the government suggested that he take his expense account to Congress for approval and payment. And this meant payment to the troops whom Arnold had personally raised. A mutiny broke out, and his soldiers held him captive in the cabin of a ship while they negotiated with a committee from Massachusetts about their back pay. They were paid, Arnold was released, and he hurried—not to Cambridge, as he had been so ordered, to settle his accounts—but to his home in New Haven.

Arnold arrived home to find that his wife, Peggy, who had grown to detest him and spurned his romantic advances, had died. Because he genuinely loved her, despite her aloofness, Arnold went into a deep depression which was further aggravated by a sudden attack of gout.

Arnold was fortunate in the depth of depression to have nearby his sister, Hannah, who stepped in immediately after Peggy's death to take care of Arnold's three young sons, ages three, six, and seven.

Anxious to settle his accounts with the Massachusetts legislature, Arnold submitted to a close scrutiny of his expense accounting during his Ticonderoga campaign. Each item was examined, and Arnold was forced time and again to defend his itemizations. Several items were disallowed, and on August 19, 1775, the board of examiners finally granted Arnold £195, less than half of what he said he had spent from his own funds.

Outraged at this slap in the face, Arnold immediately appealed to his friend in the Continental Congress, Silas Deane, for redress. Deane forwarded the full account of expenses to the appropriate congressional committee and, during January of 1776, Congress paid Arnold the £245 balance.

The meeting of Benedict Arnold and George Washington in Cambridge, Massachusetts, in August, 1775, was memorable. Each recognized in the other all the qualities that he wished for himself. Washington admired the courage and resourcefulness of his mercurial officer, while Arnold was fetched by Washington's patrician air of calmness in the face of certain defeat. Both men had lived and camped in the wilderness, and both had a thorough grasp of military strategy. Washington's concept of such strategy was the European method of traditional warfare, while Arnold was one of the first American proponents of guerrilla warfare.

The rapport between the two was immediate, and within minutes after the customary cordialities had been exchanged, Washington was asking Arnold what he thought about an invasion of Canada. And Arnold was ready with his answer.

2. Quebec

WHILE ARNOLD WAS CONFERRING with Washington, Brigadier General Richard Montgomery, a former British officer, had successfully led American troops first against Montreal —without victory—then against the British garrison at St. John's. The British surrendered, and one of the captives taken prisoner was a young officer by the name of John André.

Ever since the British and the French settled North America, military tacticians had debated ways to attack Canada. The obvious route was up Lake Champlain and through the rivers that empty into the St. Lawrence River opposite Montreal. But another route intrigued them, one followed by missionaries, explorers, and Indians. This route led through Maine along the tempestuous Kennebec River into the highlands of Maine, then over three lakes to the Dead River, then a portage of the Height of Land to the Chaudière River, and on into the St. Lawrence opposite Quebec. This route appealed to the French in Canada as a means of attacking New England, while the British recognized it as a potential for attacking Quebec and Canada.

When Arnold arrived at his headquarters, Washington had been busy planning a double-pronged invasion of Canada, with General Philip Schuyler taking a force up Lake Champlain to attack Montreal and a synchronized force moving up through Maine to attack Quebec. To Washington's mind, the British commander in Canada, Sir Guy Carleton, would have to defend either Montreal or Quebec, thus leaving an unmanned city to fall into American hands.

During their conversation together in Cambridge, Washington had been carefully examining Arnold, and he liked what he saw. This definitely was the man to lead the overland force through Maine, and Washington offered Arnold the command.

To understand Arnold's enthusiastic acceptance, it is necessary to remember that this opportunity freed him from accountability to civilian politicians, who could easily change their minds when he was halfway to Quebec. Coming from the commander in chief, General Washington, this was Benedict Arnold's first independent command. There would be no more Ethan Allens disputing his commission, no drunken Green Mountain Boys shooting at him, no more local committees cross-examining him about every penny spent.

It is important also to remember that during his prewar days as a merchant and ship captain, Arnold had sailed many times to Quebec, either up the Atlantic and the St. Lawrence or north through Lake Champlain. He knew the city well, and had many friends there. Since navigating bodies of water would be a major problem, Arnold was the perfect choice, and he also showed capabilities as a field officer.

Within hours, he was writing to various friends and conferring with a Kennebec shipbuilder about how fast two hundred bateaux could be constructed to carry six men apiece, plus provisions and equipment. Crews, guides, sup-

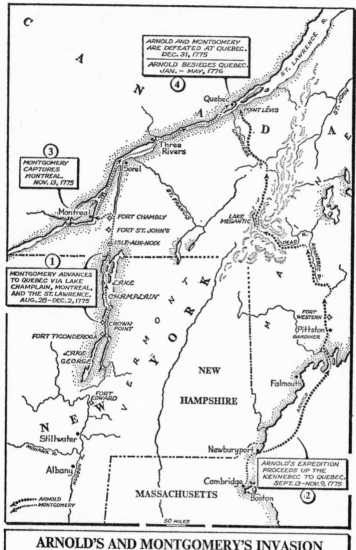

ARNOLD AND MONTGOMERY
ARE DEFEATED AT QUEBEC.
DEC. 31, 1775

ARNOLD BESIEGES QUEBEC.
JAN. – MAY, 1776

④

MONTGOMERY
CAPTURES
MONTREAL.
NOV. 13, 1775

③

MONTGOMERY ADVANCES
TO QUEBEC VIA LAKE
CHAMPLAIN, MONTREAL,
AND THE ST. LAWRENCE.
AUG. 28 – DEC. 2, 1775

①

ARNOLD'S EXPEDITION
PROCEEDS UP THE
KENNEBEC TO QUEBEC.
SEPT. 13 – NOV. 9, 1775

②

C A N A D A

ST. LAWRENCE R.

ST. JOHN

Quebec
POINT LÉVIS

Three
Rivers

Sorel

Montreal

FORT CHAMBLY
FORT ST. JOHN'S
ISLE-AUX-NOIX

ST. FRANCIS

LAKE
MEGANTIC

DEAD R.

KENNEBEC R.

LAKE
CHAMPLAIN

CROWN
POINT

FORT TICONDEROGA

LAKE
GEORGE

FORT
EDWARD

N E W

V E R M O N T

N E W   Y O R K

M A I N E

FORT
WESTERN
Pittston
GARDINER

NEW

HAMPSHIRE

Falmouth

Stillwater

MOHAWK R.

Albany

HUDSON R.

Newburyport

Cambridge

MASSACHUSETTS

Boston

ARNOLD

50 MILES

•••••• ARNOLD
———— MONTGOMERY

ARNOLD'S AND MONTGOMERY'S INVASION
OF QUEBEC
AUGUST, 1775 – JULY 1776

TRM

plies, and food had to be obtained with all possible haste, for winter was rapidly approaching Canada and New England, with enough snow and ice to stop an army of thousands.

The notice of the expedition in the general orders of September 5 called for volunteers who were woodsmen and "experienced in handling bateaus." Of the more than one thousand volunteers, few met these requirements. The crack rifle regiments under the commands of Virginia's Dan Morgan and William Thompson of Pennsylvania came closest, and they joined enthusiastically.

Some of the future heroes of the Revolution were among the first to enlist. Eleazer Oswald, who had accompanied Arnold to Ticonderoga, volunteered to serve as Arnold's secretary. Mathias Ogden of New Jersey recruited a college friend from the College of New Jersey at Princeton (now Princeton University), a nineteen-year-old youth named Aaron Burr—the man who one day would miss becoming President of the United States by one vote and who many years later would kill Alexander Hamilton in a duel.

Arnold was impatiently trying to get his troops ready to march, but he suddenly ran headlong into an obstacle that was to plague Continental commanders throughout the Revolution—money for the soldiers. The men were anxious to be paid before hiking and boating through the woods and mountains of Maine, in order to send back as much money as they could to their families. Although the riflemen—later to be denounced by the British as the "shirt-tail men, with their cursed twisted guns . . . the most fatal widow-and-orphan makers in the world"—marched immediately on orders to Newburyport, where ships would convey the troops to the mouth of the Kennebec River, several companies refused to budge until they had been paid in advance.

Knowing that each day's delay could prove disastrous to the expedition, Arnold acted promptly and saw to it that they were paid. On September 13 they marched, and on September 19 the fleet sailed, accompanied by "drums beating, fifes playing and colours flying."

The majority of these men had never been aboard a ship in the Atlantic Ocean, and the roll of the ship sent many to the sides, heaving and retching with seasickness. Simon Fobes, one of the many participants in the march to Quebec who kept a diary, experienced "such a sickness, making me feel so lifeless, so indifferent whether I lived or died!"

On September 22, the fleet anchored by Colburn's shipyard at Gardiner. There Arnold was unpleasantly surprised at the condition of the bateaux he had ordered to be built. In a letter to Washington, Arnold complained that "I found the batteaus completed, but many of them smaller than the directions given, and very badly built; of course, I have been obliged to order twenty more, to bring on the remainder of the provisions . . ."

Since most American experience with boating on the Kennebec had been on the lower, wider river, bateaux were considered ideal vessels, with their flat bottoms, flaring sides, and long, pointed bows and sterns. They were frequently used to transport heavy loads since they did not capsize easily, and they could be rowed conventionally with oars, paddled, or even poled.

However, they had never been used to transport an attack force all the way up to Canada, through rapids, around waterfalls, and over portages. For the upper journey, the lighter Indian canoe was ideal, but bateaux had been ordered and bateaux were what greeted Arnold's force.

More bad news came, this time from a scouting party that had got as far as the Dead River, where the scouts were met by the formidable Abenaki Indian chief, Natanis, who told them that he was paid by Sir Guy Carleton, military governor of Canada, to watch for any American troops. Natanis also said that the Indians under his rule were loyal to the British and would rise up against the invaders.

Arnold ignored Natanis's threat and described him to Washington as "a noted villain," adding that "very little credit, I am told, is to be given his information." This "noted villain" was later to prove an important ally and friend of the Americans.

Dan Morgan and all the riflemen were the first to move up the Kennebec, with the job of clearing a trail across the Great Carrying Place betwen the Kennebec and the Dead River. Each day a group of bateaux set off to their first rendezvous at Fort Western (now Augusta). Arnold was convinced that his troops could make the trip to Quebec in twenty days. The only unpredictable element was the arrival of winter.

From Fort Western, the men proceeded northwest, some in the bateaux, others marching along the riverbank. Soon, however, they encountered the first of several delays, when they found that they had to spend a great deal of time wading through shallow water and over rapids. At every waterfall, they had to empty the boats and hand-carry them, along with all the equipment, around the falls. Each boat weighed nearly four hundred pounds, and there were some sixty-five tons of equipment, supplies, ammunition, and food to be hauled on the aching shoulders of the volunteers.

With increasing frequency, the boatmen found themselves suddenly in whirling rapids, having to jump into icy water to keep the boats from being torn apart by the jagged rocks. Soon, however, even these efforts were not successful, and several boat bottoms were scraped, torn, and punctured.

In some cases, there was no possibility of hauling the boats ashore because the river was encased between solid vertical rock walls.

On the night of October 1, the exhausted, soaked men sank into a deep sleep, only to awaken in the morning to find their clothes frozen solid, with icy crystals signifying the arrival of winter. Carpenters worked desperately to repair the torn boats, but their efforts were largely patchwork.

Arnold encountered his first disaster when he discovered that the leaking boats had admitted enough water to seep into the casks of flour, salted fish and beef, bread, and dried vegetables, forcing Arnold to throw them away lest his troops succumb to food poisoning, diarrhea, or dropsy. In this decision he was seconded by the expedition's surgeon, Dr. Isaac Senter.

In mid-October his attack force entered the wilderness, and Arnold remained indefatigably optimistic. Only a man with Arnold's ambition and sense of destiny could have led these men from a near-frozen river into a rugged wilderness. The Great Carrying Place had been so soaked with rain that the men carrying the boats and equipment often found themselves slogging through knee-deep mud.

Meanwhile, men began to fall under exhaustion and the internal ravages of drinking water from contaminated ponds. So many became violently ill that Arnold set up a field hospital before leading the march forward to the Dead River. Although this was apparently a gentle river, some sixty yards wide, according to Arnold, its current was much stronger than his reports had indicated, and progress was very slow.

Several days of rain caused the Dead River to overflow its banks, creating lakes now two hundred yards wide. Provisions, equipment, and food were washed away, and Arnold found himself in a desperate situation. He called an emergency council of war with all available officers and outlined the critical realities of little food and worthless boats. His officers agreed as they crouched around the warming fire. After this matter-of-fact recitation, his officers would not have been surprised to hear him call for a vote on returning at once. But Benedict Arnold had traveled a long way and would travel even farther before giving up. His argument was that the rain must end soon, and the arrival of winter would harden the soggy ground and make hiking easier on the men. There was hardship ahead, but just beyond lay Quebec, the quest of the American invaders. His officers were swept up by his determination, and agreed that the only course was to push on. Arnold and some scouts galloped ahead.

Unknown to Arnold, a second council was held a few days later, and the division under Colonel Roger Enos decided to return. Arnold's command, now reduced to under 700, staggered on, fighting the river and the impossible terrain—a combination of hills, rocks, bogs, and dense woods.

And now came the critical moment. There was no food. The starving men took pieces and scraps of leather and boiled them, hoping to extract some nourishment from the juices. Boiled leather, alas, is not a source of nutrition, so the next step was to slaughter and eat any non-human creature within reach. Among these sacrifices were the personal pets of the men, especially dogs. Roast hound might not be a gourmet delicacy, but to men who have had no meat in their bellies for eight days it was succulent fare. And the bones were saved for soup.

On they drove against a new enemy, snow. As the columns pushed on toward Lake Megantic and then to the Chaudière River, the trail became dotted with the bodies of fallen soldiers. A broken ankle, a wrenched muscle, or simply fatigue meant certain death, for there was no one strong enough to care for the fallen. Officers ordered each man to shift for himself and do everything possible to remain alive.

Finally, near the end of their journey, the exhausted, starving troops were amazed to see a herd of cattle being driven toward them and canoeloads of flour and mutton coming to meet them. These had been sent back by Arnold, who also sent out horse troops to round up the still living who had fallen.

The famished troops gorged themselves. By November 3, the entire force had been well fed, but several men had ignored the cautions of moderation and died. With renewed spirit, the dwindling band pushed on, this time with Arnold accompanied by that "noted villain," Natanis, who had met Arnold and assured him that he and his followers had been watching Arnold's progress and wanted to join but were afraid they would be massacred.

On November 8, 1775, Arnold wrote to General Montgomery that he was but a short distance from Point Lévis, opposite Quebec on the St. Lawrence, and explained why it had taken him so long to make the overland journey.

> I think you had great reason to be apprehensive for me, the time I mentioned to Gen. Washington being so long since elapsed. I was not then apprised or even apprehensive of one-half of the difficulties we had to encounter . . . we have hauled our batteaux over falls, up rapid streams, over carrying places; and marched through morasses, thick woods, and over mountains, about 320 miles—many of which we had to pass several times to bring our baggage.
>
> These difficulties the soldiers have, with the greatest fortitude, surmounted. About two thirds of the detachment are, happily, arrived here and within two days' march, most of them in good health and high spirits. The other part with Col. Enos returned from the Dead River, contrary to my expectation, he having orders to send back only the sick and those that could not be furnished with provisions.

Arnold continued that he was certain that the British in Quebec knew he was coming and that all the canoes at Point Lévis had been destroyed or removed. Also, there were several armed ships anchored around Quebec. Despite what he had just undergone, Arnold's optimism is breathtaking. In a postscript to Montgomery, he adds, ". . . if you can possibly spare a regiment this way, I think the city must of course fall into our hands."

On November 8, the same day he wrote to Montgomery, Arnold proudly led his 600-plus scarecrow army onto the shore opposite Quebec. The nervous British garrison, expecting a mighty force of grave Continental soldiers, observed Arnold's command through their telescopes and smiled ironically.

(Of the 1,100 men who had started out with Arnold, only 600 reached Point Lévis, on the south bank of the St. Lawrence opposite Quebec. Instead of twenty days, as Arnold had predicted, the expedition had taken forty-five days, and they had traveled 350 miles instead of 180, which is as the crow flies from Fort Western to Point Lévis.)

But the officers were more cautious. Perhaps this was just a decoy, a ruse to lure Sir Guy Carleton's troops out onto the Plains of Abraham, a grassy meadow stretching below the Upper Town of Quebec. This is precisely what the British General Wolfe had done in 1760 to the French Commander of Quebec, Montcalm. Although both generals were mortally wounded, Wolfe's ploy had been successful and Montcalm's attack had left the Upper Town vulnerable to the British invaders.

Arnold hoped to duplicate this feat, but Carleton had read the same history books as Arnold, and he was damned if he would budge from his rock-raised citadel of the Upper Town. If Arnold wanted to storm it, fine, but Carleton would not parade his troops in front of these incredible Americans.

Unfortunately for Arnold, Carleton was his equal in strategy. In fact, Carleton was probably the most brilliant British commander in the New World; he and Benedict Arnold were evenly matched.

While Arnold and his force were fighting their way through Maine, the Army of the North had not been idle. Led first by Philip Schuyler and then by General Richard Montgomery, the Continental troops had successfully bottled up a substantial British force in St. John's, and a siege was mounted. Sir Guy Carleton—whose main force was in Quebec—sailed from Montreal with a few ships but was unsuccessful in getting near St. John's and turned back.

Montgomery finally persuaded the British commander of the embattled garrison at St. John's that, having been holed up for fifty-five days, his situation was hopeless and that decent surrender terms would be offered. On November 2, 1775, while Arnold was drawing near the St. Lawrence, the British surrendered, and one of the officers taken prisoner the following day was Lieutenant John André. Montgomery permitted the officers to retain their side arms and personal possessions, and the other men were permitted to take along their reserve supply of clothing. This decision nearly touched off a mutiny among some of Montgomery's troops, for "there was no driving it into their noodles that the clothing was really the property of the soldier, that he had paid for it," Montgomery wrote. "I wish some method could be fallen upon of engaging *gentlemen* to serve."

Montgomery marched immediately on Montreal, knowing that the Canadian attack hinged on his swift capture of the city. Despite already blustery winter weather, he managed to land above Montreal on November 12. Carleton, who had only some 200 men with him, recognized that it was the time to exercise the better part of valor and, having lost both Montreal and his small fleet, fled downriver, "dressed like a man of the people," in a rowboat whose oars were muffled to prevent detection by the Americans. However, he reached Quebec safely, and immediately sealed himself and his well-fortified and ample garrison inside the city, expecting an imminent siege.

Arnold ferried his troops across the St. Lawrence, camped them on the Plains of Abraham, and then did everything possible to provoke Carleton to send out his army. Carleton sat back and smiled, hoping that his refusal to move would ultimately provoke Arnold into a suicidal assault on the Upper Town, which the British were well prepared to defend.

On the night of November 19, having learned that a force of 800 British troops were about to attack them, Arnold led his men on another cold march some twenty miles north to Point aux Trembles (now Neuville), where they remained for two weeks. During this time, Carleton successfully made his re-entry into Quebec, bad news for the American forces, who now seemed as remote from Quebec as they had been at the mouth of the Kennebec.

However, on December 2, Arnold's force was joined by Montgomery, who brought 300 men, plus—most important—a large supply of British winter clothing which they had captured at Montreal.

Richard Montgomery was one of those charismatic men—not unlike Benedict Arnold—who immediately inspire men they command. He addressed the troops and applauded their incredible march, and they showed their enthusiasm by cheering the young general.

Writing to Schuyler, Montgomery said, "I find Colonel Arnold's corps an exceeding fine one, inured to fatigue . . . there is a style of discipline among them much superior to what I have been used to see in this campaign."

Cheered by Montgomery's arrival, Arnold suggested an immediate return to Quebec. Upon their arrival, Montgomery, surveying the frozen land, realized that a classic siege was out of the question, since earthworks would be impossible. Also, he didn't have an engineer to design them. Instead, he resorted to bravado by calling on Carleton to surrender before he was starved out. Montgomery's summons was pure bluff; Carleton knew it as such, and treated it with contempt. Twice earlier, Arnold had attempted to send into Quebec a messenger under a white flag with a summons to surrender, but the British had merely fired muskets and cannon at him.

So Montgomery hired a local woman to bring his summons to Carleton by going to the city gate and saying she had an important message for the commander. Once in Carleton's presence, she told him that it was a message from the American commander. With what can only be described today as *style*, Carleton ordered a drummer into the room, and had him take up the unopened envelope with a pair of tongs and drop it into the fire. He sent the woman back with instructions to tell Montgomery that he would accept no messages from rebels. Several days later, Montgomery wrote another letter intended to scare Carleton into submission, and again sent it by a local woman. This time, Carleton was determined to put a stop to this rebel nonsense. He had the woman thrown in jail overnight, and then drummed her ignominiously out of the city, with Carleton's scorn for a reply.

This little war of nerves between two tough military commanders illustrates that Carleton, who had barely escaped capture by Montgomery a few days earlier—now that he was safe in his citadel—could behave arrogantly when, in fact, he was probably quite scared.

This battle of wits between Carleton and Montgomery, and later between Carleton and Arnold, apparently was to the British general's liking, for years later he was to befriend his old foe, Benedict Arnold, when all of London turned its back on him.

Arnold and Montgomery ordered their men to put

sprigs of hemlock in their hats in order to distinguish friend from foe. On December 27, snow started to fall and the troops assembled, but then the snow suddenly blew off to the east and the attack had to be postponed. The commanders decided that it would be simpler for both of their forces to enter the Lower Town from opposite sides and work their way up to the citadel of the Upper Town.

In deciding to storm the city, both Montgomery and Arnold laid themselves open to accusations of bad generalship. But they had to take some action before the first of the year, when a large portion of their men would leave for home. Storming a citadel like Quebec was impractical, but it just might work during a December blizzard. At best, the Americans would seize the city. At worst, they would fail, but no one could then accuse Montgomery and Arnold of not trying. Also, even if they achieved only partial success, that might induce some of the volunteers to stay on a bit longer.

On the night of December 31, the snow, which had been falling lightly, suddenly grew into a blizzard. Arnold made a personal inspection of his men in the houses where they were quartered, delivered brief encouragements, and did his best to excite them for the impending battle.

Assembling his men, Arnold marched them swiftly into the driving snowstorm, approaching the Lower Town from the northeast, while Montgomery's force marched from the southwest. Just as both forces neared the entry to the Lower Town, a rocket cut through the air, followed by two more. This was the signal for all the church bells in Quebec to start ringing, and ring they did.

Discarding silence, Arnold waved his sword and spurred his men to a charge. Working his way into a nar-

row street in the Lower Town, Arnold knew that at the
top of this street was a barricade where the British had
certainly planted a cannon, well equipped with canister shot
—hunks of iron, nails, and other lethal objects which could
mow down an advancing column much more effectively
than a single cannon ball. Canister shot resembled today's
shotgun pellets in its scattering effect. Arnold knew that
he would have to take this cannon before he could move
on to the Upper Town, so he ordered a charge. He could
see the flash of the cannon powder seconds before the
explosion roared down, accompanied by flying bits of
metal. Arnold was untouched, and he shouted for his men
to follow him. Suddenly, musket fire poured down on all
sides of his force from the surrounding houses.

Arnold was almost at the barricade when a sharp pain
seared his lower left leg. Thinking he might have been
grazed, he continued the charge, but suddenly he could go
no farther and leaned against a house.

"Go on, God damn it, lads!" he screamed at those
who hesitated, when they saw their leader falter, blood
oozing over the top of his boot. "Follow Morgan and take
the town!"

Arnold waited until Morgan and his men had penetrated the barricade and started to move to the Upper
Town before he allowed himself to be helped back toward
camp by two men. Some of the troops passing him stopped
in uncertainty, but Arnold rallied them with his usual
encouragement. "Rush on, lads, rush on!"

Arnold was carried with the rest of the wounded to
the Catholic convent outside the walls, which had been
appropriated as a field hospital. There his friend and
surgeon, Isaac Senter, discovered that a portion of a bullet

had ricocheted from a rock and had entered his leg mid-way between knee and ankle and had lodged in his heel. Senter gave his illustrious patient a stiff jolt of rum and offered him a musket ball to bite on, which Arnold refused. It was a relatively simple operation to remove the fragment, but it was done without benefit of anesthesia, and Arnold's suffering must have been excruciating.

While recovering from the operation, Arnold received a stream of messengers who reported that Montgomery had been killed, that Arnold's men had penetrated the British barricades but then disappeared, and that the British were assembling a force to attack the field hospital and bayonet the wounded.

Arnold sat up in his bed and roared that every man should equip himself with firearms in order to defend himself to the last. One can only imagine the reaction of the nuns who were treating the wounded. The rumor of a British attack proved to be false.

As more and more American troops withdrew, Arnold passed on his leadership to his second-in-command and fell into a delirium-racked sleep.

Meanwhile, Morgan had led his men over the barricades and swiftly captured a houseful of British soldiers. The invading force pushed into the Lower Town, where they were joined by additional troops. They stormed another barricade, only to be thrown back by musket and cannon fire. Morgan's only hope lay in the immediate arrival of Montgomery's forces, with which the Americans conceivably could have battered their way into the Upper Town and victory. But Montgomery had not come, and Morgan's men, surrounded now by British troops advancing on them with their dreaded bayonets, threw down their arms and surrendered. Morgan, his back against a wall and tears of impotent rage streaming down his craggy face, waved his sword at the advancing bayonets and yelled hoarsely, "If you want my sword, you'll have to take it from me!"

When the British threatened to shoot, and his men were pleading with him not to throw away his life, the towering Virginian spotted a priest in the crowd and called him forward.

"Are you a priest? Then I give my sword to you. But not a scoundrel of these cowards shall take it out of my hands."

Montgomery's fate had been briefer than Morgan's.

After cutting their way through two barricades, Montgomery's men followed their general past a blockhouse and toward what appeared to be a fortified house. In his eagerness, Montgomery did not wait for the rest of his troops to pull themselves through the breached barricades and the snowdrifts. He and two dozen others moved forward cautiously, all the while watched by the British and American Tory volunteers inside the house, holding their fire until they were certain to cut down the invaders, a tactic the rebels had used to such good advantage earlier at Bunker Hill. When Montgomery, Burr, and several other officers were within a few yards of the house, all hell broke loose. Cannon and muskets poured canister shot and bullets into the Americans, killing Montgomery immediately, along with a dozen others. Aaron Burr and two or three others escaped unhurt.

The remnant of Montgomery's command retreated, part of it captured by Carleton's troops. When Benedict Arnold recovered enough to resume command, he found that after more than 100 militiamen whose enlistments were up on January 1 had departed, he had fewer than 500 men left in his command.

By April 2, more men augmented the tiny American force, and Benedict Arnold, commissioned a brigadier general by Congress in recognition of his incredible march and battle, turned over command to General David Wooster and moved down to Montreal. Surprised by what he found at Quebec, Wooster praised Arnold's blockade of Quebec and wrote to Washington that "General Arnold has, to his great honour, kept up the blockade with such a handful of men that the story, when told hereafter, will be scarcely credited."

Prophetic words. Throw him into the midst of a battle, and no matter how heavy the odds against him, Benedict Arnold's determination inevitably radiated enthusiasm and renewed vigor to his tattered troops. He achieved miracles during the American Revolution, miracles which rarely find their way into textbooks and popular histories but are confined to the laborious research of the detached historian.

Had Quebec been captured, Arnold's march would have been given proper credit as one of the most famous military marches in history. It was in any case one of the great achievements of the Continental army, and, coupled with his later exploits on Lake Champlain and at Saratoga, it justifies the esteem of Arnold's contemporaries for his military leadership.

After learning of what Arnold had done, Joseph Warren wrote to Samuel Adams, "Arnold has made a march that may be compared to Hannibal's or Xenophon's," and Thomas Jefferson concurred in this opinion.

One final accolade deserves to be quoted.

"The march of Col. Arnold and his troops is one of the greatest exploits recorded in the annals of nations."

This was the opinion of the British historian, Murray.

With the coming of the spring thaw to the St. Lawrence, the power of Sir Guy Carleton's forces, augmented by a fresh batch of British soldiers under the command of Carleton's new second-in-command, General John Burgoyne, swept the Americans from Canada. The last man to leave Canadian soil was Benedict Arnold. He stood by the shore of St. John's, waiting until he heard the thundering hoofs of the advance cavalry. In the distance, Arnold could see red coats and flashing steel. He removed the saddle from his horse, placed it in a canoe, put his gun to his horse's head, and shot the animal dead, lest it fall into British hands. With that gesture, he paddled from St. John's down the river and into Lake Champlain, defeated yet victorious.

Arnold paddled away from Canada on June 18, 1776, but this was not the last the British were to see of him that year.

3. The Father of the American Navy

THIS CHAPTER is not about John Paul Jones or any of the other seafaring leaders of American forces in the Atlantic. No, it is about the man who got away from the British that day in 1776, a man whose capture was ardently desired by the British Colonial Secretary, Lord Germain. Displaying more insight than he was to show during the remainder of the Revolution, Germain wrote to Burgoyne, in response to the British officer's report of the recent expedition against the rebels, "I am sorry Arnold escaped. I think he has shown himself the most enterprising man among the rebels."

Perhaps Germain understood that a man of Arnold's energy, resourcefulness, and tactical brilliance would continue to be a serious threat to His Majesty's forces until he was safely clapped in irons or killed.

The British, having driven the Americans from Canada, now proceeded with their plans to sail into Lake Champlain, then down the Hudson from Albany to New York City. A glance at the map will show the importance of this north-south waterway to both sides in the conflict. Seizure of it would have the effect of fragmenting the colonies, and this was the ambition of the British high command in London.

Between June 19 and October 10, Arnold did not disturb the British, for he was too busy—at Washington's request—constructing a fleet at Skenesboro (today, Whitehall, New York) at the extreme southern end of Lake Champlain. Knowing that Carleton would have to take apart and reconstruct his heavier vessels, which could not pass through the rapids of the Sorel River and which were too large to be dragged overland by oxen, as could flatboats, and bateaux, Arnold worked feverishly to construct a defensive fleet to augment the ships the Americans already commanded on the lake: the schooners *Royal Savage*, *Liberty*, and *Revenge*, and the sloop *Enterprise*. All but the *Revenge*—which had been built by the Americans—had been captured on the lake.

The task Arnold faced was to get enough skilled ship carpenters, sailmakers, and riggers, not to mention woodsmen to fell the trees. Also needed were the materials with which to construct a fleet. Those skilled naval workers who had joined the army were immediately hustled north to Skenesboro, where they were joined by men from the coastal seaports of New England and the middle Atlantic states. Four row galleys and nine gondolas were constructed in record time during those four frantic months. Turning over the actual supervision of the building to General David Waterbury, Arnold spent his time planning his attack on the British, gathering intelligence reports about the speed of Carleton's reconstruction of the British fleet, and rushing around the shipyard, encouraging the workers.

The row galleys, which were around seventy feet long and eighteen feet wide, carried eighty men apiece, while the smaller gondolas, measuring forty-five feet in length, carried forty-five men each. Each type had sails, but several

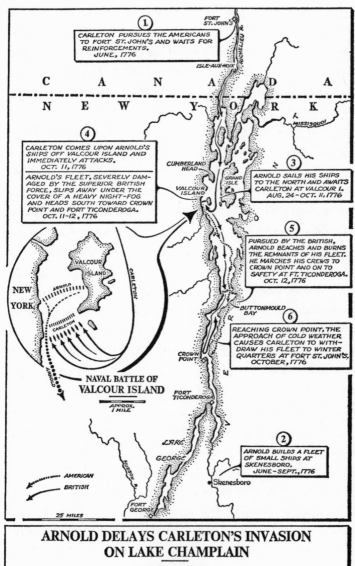

1. CARLETON PURSUES THE AMERICANS TO FORT ST. JOHN'S AND WAITS FOR REINFORCEMENTS. JUNE, 1776

4. CARLETON COMES UPON ARNOLD'S SHIPS OFF VALCOUR ISLAND AND IMMEDIATELY ATTACKS. OCT. 11, 1776

ARNOLD'S FLEET, SEVERELY DAMAGED BY THE SUPERIOR BRITISH FORCE, SLIPS AWAY UNDER THE COVER OF A HEAVY NIGHT-FOG AND HEADS SOUTH TOWARD CROWN POINT AND FORT TICONDEROGA. OCT. 11-12, 1776

3. ARNOLD SAILS HIS SHIPS TO THE NORTH AND AWAITS CARLETON AT VALCOUR I. AUG. 24-OCT. 11, 1776

5. PURSUED BY THE BRITISH, ARNOLD BEACHES AND BURNS THE REMNANTS OF HIS FLEET. HE MARCHES HIS CREWS TO CROWN POINT AND ON TO SAFETY AT FT. TICONDEROGA. OCT. 12, 1776

6. REACHING CROWN POINT, THE APPROACH OF COLD WEATHER CAUSES CARLETON TO WITHDRAW AT WINTER QUARTERS AT FORT ST. JOHN'S. OCTOBER, 1776

2. ARNOLD BUILDS A FLEET OF SMALL SHIPS AT SKENESBORO. JUNE-SEPT., 1776

NAVAL BATTLE OF **VALCOUR ISLAND**

APPROX. 1 MILE

AMERICAN
BRITISH

25 MILES

CANADA

NEW YORK

FORT ST. JOHN'S
RICHELIEU R.
ISLE-AUX-NOIX
MISSISQUOI
CUMBERLAND HEAD
GRAND ISLE
VALCOUR ISLAND
NEW YORK
ARNOLD
CARLETON
BUTTONMOULD BAY
CROWN POINT
FORT TICONDEROGA
L. GEORGE
HUDSON R.
Skenesboro
FORT GEORGE

ARNOLD DELAYS CARLETON'S INVASION ON LAKE CHAMPLAIN

JUNE – OCTOBER
1776

TRM

sets of oars were provided in case the wind failed at a
critical moment. During the construction, the American
workers were delighted by the arrival of fresh beef and
other provisions, including rum and wine. The Declaration
of Independence was read to the workers and troops on
July 28, and it was greeted by loud cheering.

The British fleet nearing completion just north of Lake
Champlain outgunned and outmanned the American fleet
to such a degree that for Arnold to even attempt to delay
the British was almost suicidal. But the main reason for the
fleet was to stall the British and slow the inevitable invasion.
Benedict Arnold was never awed by superior forces, and
by mid-September he had his fleet in the waters of Lake
Champlain and the crews undergoing naval maneuvers.

Arnold sailed to the sheltered stretch of water on the
west side of Valcour Island, with the New York shore on
the left. Valcour Island (opposite Burlington, Vermont)
formed an excellent shelter for his fleet, which he arranged
in a half-moon position. He sent scouting ships scurrying
around the island to warn the Americans of the first on-
slaught of the British invasion.

The war in the north had by now settled down to a
duel of wits and armaments between two extraordinary
generals, Sir Guy Carleton and Benedict Arnold. Sir Guy
is rarely mentioned in popular histories as the man who
held Quebec, chased the Americans out of Canada, and
came closer than any other British general to splitting the
colonies in half and squelching the Revolution. Carleton's
genius has been eclipsed by the flashiness of his second-in-
command and later successor, "Gentleman Johnny" Burgoyne. Carleton was prepared to smash through the American forces at Crown Point and Ticonderoga, and he was

better equipped and his strategy better planned than Burgoyne's the following year, when the Americans had had a year's time to develop their strength and defeat Burgoyne at Saratoga.

There was only one man standing between Carleton and victory—Arnold. No other American officer was more highly respected—and feared—by the British army commanders than Benedict Arnold. He had a reputation for persistence, for surprise, for recoiling back after seeming defeat, for inspiring his untrained militia and regulars to miraculous recovery and renewed energy.

Throughout the summer of 1776, Carleton's spies brought reports that Arnold was constructing a fleet to oppose the British as they sailed down the lake. The reports of the numbers and sizes of the ships in the American flotilla made Carleton smile, for his ships were powerful enough to blast them to pieces the moment they hove in sight. The only flaw in his plan, as Sir Guy probably recognized, was that the American ships would be under the command of Benedict Arnold. Ordinarily, generals make rotten admirals, and seamen do not fare well in land battles. But Carleton was well aware of Arnold's seagoing experience, and he wondered what surprises the rebel would spring on him.

Carleton set sail on the morning of October 11 into the lake, but he neglected to send ahead any scouting boats to peek behind Valcour Island and discover the rebel fleet. A strong northerly wind filled the sails of the British ships, and they sailed past Valcour, not spotting the American ships until they had passed two miles south of the island.

Carleton knew he could not continue southward and let Arnold's fleet attack St. John's and wipe out his supply line. Ordering his fleet to turn about, Carleton found that the north wind was no longer friendly. Tacking clumsily toward Valcour Bay, the British ships inched their way to some 350 yards of the American half-moon position, and then, around noon, both rows of ships erupted in gunfire.

They thundered away at each other, sometimes not even knowing where to aim, because of the thick concentrations of smoke from the cannons. Aboard the schooner *Maria*, Sir Guy ordered her sister ship, the *Carleton*, to hit the enemy with a broadside. But Arnold, aboard the *Congress* (one of the new ships), ordered his ships to concentrate their firing on the *Carleton*.

While the battle raged, Arnold was racing about like a demon, personally sighting the guns on the *Congress* and shouting encouragement to his "brave lads."

Ships sank, others listed. Sails were shredded and masts broken on both sides of the firing. The Americans were clearly taking a beating, but they were standing fast. Blood flowed on the decks, and surgeons worked to amputate shattered limbs, remove musket balls, sew up wounds, and stanch the flow of blood.

As evening approached, the British fleet fell back into a line commanding the southern entrance to Valcour Bay. Arnold called a council of war on his flagship, and the American situation was examined dispassionately. Several ships had sunk or were too ravaged to remain manned. Sixty men had been killed or wounded, and the ammunition supply was almost gone. Looking through a porthole, the officers could see the gondola *Philadelphia* sink as the fog rolled in. [This is the same ship that, raised from the bottom of the lake and restored, is now a popular exhibit at the Smithsonian Institution in Washington, D.C.] Arnold asked the opinion of his officers, and they all agreed that there were not enough ships, men, or ammunition to resume the fight in the morning, and it appeared that they would have to surrender or be wiped out.

Pacing the cabin tensely, Arnold scarcely heard these words. Surrender he was not about to do, not after all he had achieved. He had already delayed the British, sank some of their ships, and killed several persons. Also, he had shown both British and Americans that the rebels could fight. Suddenly, the fog gave him inspiration. Those who have seen the fog that frequently covers the northern end of Lake Champlain at dusk can understand Arnold's sudden excitement. The fog is so thick that visibility is limited to no more than a dozen feet.

Springing to the table and his maps, Arnold outlined his plan of escape, to slip between the British and the western shore. To carry out this boldness, Arnold ordered each ship to hang a single lantern in its stern, hooded so as to be seen only by the ship immediately behind it.

His voice rising in excitement, Arnold convinced his officers, and they returned to their ships to prepare for immediate departure. Strict silence was to be maintained, and all lights except the one in the stern were extinguished.

Once darkness was complete, the *Trumbull* raised just enough sail to move gently along the bank, with the small craft following and Arnold's ship, the *Congress,* bringing up the rear. The Americans could not see the British ships in the fog, but they could hear the noises of hammers and pumps and talking. Every American aboard the creeping fleet was aware that the least sound would expose them to the full power of the British armada, and when Arnold's flagship cleared the British fleet, there was considerable mopping of brows and relaxed breathing. Arnold had done it again, by God, and no one aboard these vessels would ever forget it. As soon as they were out of hearing range, the American ships broke out the oars and the pumps and moved as rapidly as possible in the direction of Crown Point and Ticonderoga.

By dawn, several of the least damaged ships had made considerable progress down the lake, but the others, including Arnold's flagship, had made only eight miles to Schuyler's Island. At daybreak Carleton discovered the escape of the rebels and was enraged, ordering an immediate pursuit. But then, as his ships neared Schuyler's Island, which the last of the American ships were leaving, Carleton remembered that in his haste he had forgotten to give appropriate orders to his forces marching along the west bank of the lake. Furious at this error, Carleton turned back to Valcour Bay, dispatched orders, and immediately set sail with his full fleet in hot pursuit of Arnold.

The slower rebel galleys were rowing into a south wind, whereas the British were suddenly blessed with a strong northerly wind and moved swiftly down on the stragglers. As the British ships drew near, Arnold opened fire on them, but as the American ships passed Split Rock, the British overtook them and raked them with cannon and grapeshot. The *Washington* was captured, and two others ran ashore and were abandoned, then captured by the British. But the northerly wind caught up with the *Congress* and four gondolas just as the British approached within accurate firing distance. For more than two hours, three large British ships and four smaller ones thundered away at the *Congress*, but Arnold refused to surrender.

Arnold ordered his flagship and the gondolas to row

into the wind to the Vermont shore, thwarting the British, who had to beat to windward, making little progress. Arnold ordered his boats beached on Buttonmould Bay, and he then set them on fire, with their flags still flying. The British, sensitive to this dramatic gesture of defiance, were unable to do anything more than sustain a cannonade. Arnold was the last to leave the *Congress*, and as that battered command ship went up in a sheet of flames, he leaped to the shore, the last man to leave his ships.

Arnold's men hiked overland ten miles south, then were ferried across to Crown Point, where they found the five ships left from their fleet. Realizing that Crown Point could not hold off Carleton, Arnold and the rest retreated rapidly to Ticonderoga.

Just as they reached the powerful fortress, several British rowboats approached under a flag of truce, and out stepped General Waterbury and the hundred-man crew of the captured *Washington*. In a magnanimous gesture, Carleton had paroled them.

As the freed Americans were praising the generosity of their captor, Sir Guy was quietly studying his options. Carleton could see through his telescope the virtual impregnability of Ticonderoga. A frontal attack would be suicidal, for the star-shaped fortress was equipped with enough cannon to blow the British fleet out of the water. To mount a siege would consume valuable days, and Carleton had already been delayed by his need to construct extra vessels to offset Arnold's fleet. Arnold's surprise at Valcour Island and the subsequent chase halfway down Lake Champlain left Carleton dubious about continuing the campaign into the winter, so far from his home base. And God only knew what maneuvers the incredible Arnold might execute, such as severing the British supply line in the north and then sweeping southward with a new fleet (Why not? It only took him three months to build the first one!) to trap the British between the rebel forces.

Carleton, who had come so far, realized that Arnold had indeed slowed him down to the point where prudence dictated a withdrawal to St. John's, where preparations could be made for an early spring campaign.

It was this withdrawal, of course, that gave the colonial forces time to breathe and to prepare for the British assault the following year, culminating at Saratoga, where once again Benedict Arnold would defeat the British.

Lake Champlain today is as still as it was before the Revolution. Although parts of it are polluted, the waters swirling along the rocky New York shore opposite Valcour Island are clear. As one stands alongside a hidden little historical marker noting the date and the battle as the sun sets on a cool October afternoon, one can almost hear again the roar of the cannons and see the smoke billowing over the water as Arnold's tight half-moon fleet traded fire with the British.

Because so much of Lake Champlain is unchanged, it is possible to see it, with the distant mountains on either side, as it was in 1776, when Sir Guy Carleton and Benedict Arnold fought one of the most remarkable naval battles in modern history. Buttonmould Bay, which is now called Button Bay, is virtually deserted. No historical markers point out its significance, and wild grass grows just as it did when Arnold beached his boats and set fire to them, their colors flying. Once again, Arnold had failed to defeat the British, but once again his loss was more than a victory.

Alfred Thayer Mahan, an authority on naval history, summarized Arnold's achievements on Lake Champlain succinctly.

That the Americans were strong enough to impose the capitulation of Saratoga was due to the invaluable year of delay secured to them in 1776 by their little navy on Lake Champlain, created by the indomitable energy, and handled with the indomitable courage of the traitor, Benedict Arnold.

Even Admiral Mahan could not avoid throwing in that red-flag word while prasing Arnold.

As one follows Benedict Arnold's career from 1775 at Ticonderoga until October, 1777, when he fought his last battle as an American general, one recognizes that his achievements were considerable, his heroism and daring unquestioned, and even his recklessness that of a genius.

From his storming of Quebec to his capture of the Breymann redoubt, Arnold bore the physical pain of a wounded left leg. On horseback, the pain was not as severe. But on board his flagship, he had to limp painfully from gun to gun in order to sight them.

Until the victory at Saratoga and his forced retirement from a field command, Arnold was the most respected and feared rebel officer in the eyes of the British.

Surrendering to Horatio Gates at Saratoga, Burgoyne said, "The fortunes of war, General Gates, have made me your prisoner." But in writing to Sir Henry Clinton in New York, Burgoyne stated flatly, "It was his doing." There is no question whom Burgoyne meant.

4. Arnold's Enemies Gather

No MILITARY COMMANDER is universally beloved. Even if his troops love him, he is likely to have made enemies among his fellow officers. And the greater the general, the more enemies he has.

The old platitude about George Washington commanding the esteem and love of all who served with or under him is ludicrous. Washington was heartily detested by many of the enlisted men, who considered his ideas about discipline barbaric (a view shared by Washington's good friend, the Marquis de Lafayette). Washington thought nothing of sentencing men to be whipped, tortured, shot, or hanged. The commander in chief never seemed to understand that when a man volunteers to fight in an army, he is not likely to feel well treated if he is tied to a whipping post for thirty-nine lashes with a leather whip.

(Some of Washington's favorite instruments of discipline have been faithfully reproduced at the New Windsor Cantonment at Vail's Gate, New York. In this restored camp are the "horse" and the whipping post. The "horse" was an ingenious device that reduced the hardiest men to tears and left many of them crippled for life. It resembled a standard carpenter's horse—a long piece of wood supported by two sets of legs—except that it stood some ten feet above the ground. The miscreant sentenced to ride on the "horse" was forced to straddle the narrow crosspiece while two heavy cannon balls were tied to his feet. If his offense was particularly heinous, his arms might be tied to prevent him from easing the excruciating agony. Ultimately, Washington concluded that such a punishment was inhuman, and abandoned it.)

Resentment against Washington was not confined to the lower ranks. There were many who thought they should have got Washington's job, including Major Generals Horatio Gates and Charles Lee, and they never tired of telling their feelings to any who would listen. Washington was no saint, and in many ways he was a terrible general. However, his unshakable loyalty stood as an example for every other American who wanted to be rid of British rule.

Like Washington, Benedict Arnold had more than his share of enemies. Any man who moves so swiftly and strikes with unerring brilliance is not going to be popular among conservative officers.

At the conclusion of the Valcour Island naval battle, Arnold was riding high in the esteem of those officers who, in his mind, counted. The two generals whose feud over command of the Army of the North would come close to ruining the Continental cause, Horatio Gates and Philip Schuyler, were both admirers of Arnold. In less than a year, Gates and Arnold would be at each other's throat, while Schuyler's friendship toward Arnold would become useless.

It is worth pausing a moment to consider the sharply different characters of the two men jockeying for command of the Army of the North. Horatio Gates and Philip Schuyler were miles apart in personality, upbringing, and life style. Gates, the son of English servants, discovered early in his career in the British army that his parentage would forever hold him back from promotion and advancement. In the eighteenth-century British army, only those of noble family or with newly acquired riches could hope to advance. Gates left the British army in disgust, moved to the American colonies, and happened to be available to take command of the army when the Revolution broke out. Although Washington was chosen by Congress to be commander in chief, Gates was one of the first men named a major general.

One of his fellow major generals was the aristocratic Philip Schuyler, a wealthy landowner who had several houses in and around Albany along the upper Hudson River. Schuyler had had military training and generally knew what he was doing. His efficiency was crippled, however, by the dawning of the democratic revolution.

Long before the French Revolution overthrew the nobility and the concept of hereditary powers and rights, democratic concepts had taken hold in the American colonies. Councils of war too often became town meetings, with every soldier feeling he had a right to speak up and discuss the pros and cons of a particular military action. Such a notion was to plague officers like Benedict Arnold, who operate on instinct, shrewdness, and cleverness. Arnold could never have achieved what he did had he called for a democratic discussion and vote. This attitude was to win him enemies.

Unlike Arnold, Philip Schuyler was a born aristocrat, and he behaved like one, looking down his long nose at men he considered to be his inferiors. He was born to command, just as the lesser-born were destined to follow their superiors and obey.

At the outbreak of the Revolution, New England was a hotbed of democratic leveling, with militia groups electing their own officers. When men from Massachusetts, Maine, and New Hampshire came into contact with a patrician like Schuyler, they did not hesitate to tell him and his officers where to shove their aristocracy.

Thus, Schuyler was highly unpopular with the New Englanders, but eagerly followed by his New York regiments. On the other hand, the plebeian Gates, who had risen from the lower classes, was well-liked by the New Englanders.

Benedict Arnold, who combined the traits of both Gates and Schuyler, was befriended by both men. During the year between Valcour Island and Saratoga, Arnold was to unwittingly show such partiality toward Schuyler and his cronies as to infuriate Gates and turn this former friend into a bitter enemy. Also, at the time of the Valcour Island battle, Gates was officially in command of the Army of the North, and he had specifically ordered Arnold not to engage the British but to lead his fleet safely back to Ticonderoga, which Gates was convinced could withstand any British assault.

Arnold's disobedience of Gates's orders happened to be so spectacular that Gates publicly praised Arnold while mentally noting that Arnold was not to be trusted, except where suicidal heroism and recklessness were the only course.

"It has pleased Providence to preserve General Arnold," Gates wrote in his report. "Few men have met with so many hairbreadth escapes in so short a space of time. . . . Such magnanimous behavior will establish the fame of the American arms throughout the world."

With the conclusion of the Valcour Island battle, Arnold, who had been grumbling about wanting time to himself to relax and forget about the war, became restless. What the thunderous ovation is to the actor, the booming cannon and crackling muskets are to creative military minds like Benedict Arnold. Considering these factors, it becomes easier to understand what happened to Benedict Arnold after the last cannon was fired at him in Buttonmould Bay. The man was restless, eager to have at the British again. But his restlessness had a year to fester and grow before he would tear himself loose from inactivity and once again ride into battle.

During that year, a number of personal grudges and complaints against Arnold had time to surface and to harass him to the point of fury.

One John Brown, who had been cursing Arnold under his breath during the march on Quebec, loudly denounced Arnold to Gates and demanded his arrest for assorted crimes.

Major John Brown was a smooth-talking young lawyer, a graduate of Yale and related by marriage to Arnold's cousin, Oliver Arnold, of Rhode Island. Joined by Colonel James Easton, a loud tavern-keeper, Brown seemed destined to conduct an intensive vendetta against Arnold. And since Easton and Brown had influential friends in the Massachusetts legislature as well as in the Continental Congress, they successfully sowed the first seeds of doubt and distrust in those two governmental bodies against Arnold.

Both Brown and Easton had been denied promotion in Canada by General Montgomery because of unresolved charges against them of plundering the baggage of British officers taken captive by the Americans. And Arnold supported this decision after Montgomery's death.

Brown compiled a list of Arnold's deeds, starting with the march to Quebec and concluding with the loss of the Champlain fleet following Valcour Island, and twisted the facts in such a way as to make Arnold appear the blackest villain imaginable. He presented these charges to Arnold's good friend and the commander of the Army of the North, General Philip Schuyler. Reading them with astonishment, Schuyler looked up coldly at Brown and told him that if he didn't get out of headquarters with his absurd charges, Schuyler would have Brown arrested and prosecuted for "violent and ill-founded complaints."

Brown persisted and when Gates officially took command in the north, he re-presented his indictment of Arnold. Gates bluntly refused to appoint a court-martial to study such specious charges. However, he knew too well what friends Brown and his cohort, Easton had in the government in Philadelphia, so he was forced to forward the accusations to Congress.

Meanwhile, Arnold accompanied Gates to lead four regiments to join Washington, who, when last heard from, had been camped with his army in New Jersey after his speedy eviction from Manhattan by the British. Halfway to New York, the two generals learned that Washington had been forced to retreat through New Jersey to the Pennsylvania side of the Delaware River, opposite Trenton.

They were almost at Washington's new headquarters when Arnold received orders dispatching him to New England, a British fleet having been sighted off Providence. Arnold was anxious to see Washington again, for the first time since he had set off for Quebec, and, with Gates's blessing, he hurried on to the American camp. Arnold had also wanted to proceed to Philadelphia to confer with congressmen about the slurs on his character and integrity, but to Washington's delight, he agreed to move immediately to New England.

At this point in the Revolution, Washington's spirits were at their lowest. Like many men, he was a victim of depression, and during the dreary days just before Christmas, 1776, Washington wondered whether his cause might indeed be lost.

He had suffered major defeats, particularly in the Battle of Long Island at Brooklyn, but had magically escaped the British. He knew his own generalship was largely to blame, but he had been beset by incompetent lieutenants and an army which constantly dwindled as disgusted soldiers returned to their farms and mills.

It is possible to imagine the warm glow Washington felt when Arnold arrived at headquarters. They spent four days together, no doubt reviewing the entire Quebec and Lake Champlain campaigns. The brandy and Madeira probably flowed freely although Arnold shunned excessive drinking because he had seen his father disintegrate into alcoholism when confronted with failure in Connecticut.

What warmed Washington more than the liquor was this visible proof that starving, unpaid soldiers could be held together through a nasty winter in a futile blockade of Quebec. Perhaps wishing that he possessed some of

Arnold's magnetism and enthusiasm, the commander in chief questioned Arnold closely about his achievements.

The night before Arnold was to leave for New England, the two spent several hours discussing a possible surprise attack across the Delaware on the British barracks at Trenton. This was a concept which immediately appealed to Arnold, and his vigorous encouragement may have been the final nudge Washington needed to carry out his superb attack on Trenton, just four days after Arnold had left.

The Battle of Trenton was the first real military victory for the Continental army under Washington's command. Until then, all the American victories had been guerrilla-style, undirected attacks on the British, as at Concord and Bunker Hill. Now Washington could report to Congress with pride, and American ambassadors at foreign courts could cite a significant victory. It was Trenton that started France thinking about possible official support of the American rebels, and it was Saratoga that made it official.

Arnold moved north, accompanied by Colonel John Trumbull, son of the governor of Connecticut and destined to become one of the Revolution's greatest artists, with his canvases hanging in the Capitol in Washington and in many other museums and collections. Since the British seemed to be dozing at Newport, Arnold obtained permission from Washington to visit his family in New Haven, whom he had not seen in eighteen months.

He was given a triumphant reception as he rode from city to city on the way to New Haven. Cannon were discharged in his honor, and veterans of the Maine march and the Quebec battle who had been captured and later exchanged by the British, limped out to meet him. His good friend John Lamb, who had lost an eye while commanding the artillery at Quebec, wept as he hugged the Eagle of the North.

After an ego-soothing reception from his former neighbors in New Haven, and after a joyous reunion with his sister, Hannah, and his three sons, Arnold set about to remedy injustices towards his friends and fellow soldiers.

With a thousand-dollar loan, he gave Lamb enough money to raise a regiment of artillery, with Lamb in command as colonel and Eleazer Oswald, another old friend and his secretary during the march to Quebec, as lieutenant colonel.

Arnold arrived in Providence on January 12, 1777, after spending a week with his family. There he reported to General Joseph Spencer, who was technically his superior but whom Washington regarded as merely a figurehead.

One of the top American commanders, General Nathanael Greene, himself a Rhode Islander, wrote to the governor of that state that Arnold and Spencer would be taking command of all forces, and added, "Arnold is a fine, spirited fellow, and an active general."

On December 8, 1776, the British settled into Newport as a winter encampment, according to the unwritten rule that gentlemen do not make war during the winter. Benedict Arnold was bound by no such rules, and he set about to raise an army from Rhode Island, Massachusetts, and New Hampshire.

Traveling to Boston in order to recruit battalions, he was received with surprising warmth by the notoriously snobbish Bostonians. The tradesman who, two years earlier, would have been snubbed in the drawing rooms, was now fussed over and lionized by the finest of society. He promptly became the guest of honor at parties, the grandest of which was given by Mrs. Henry Knox, wife of Washington's commander of artillery and a member of Boston society by virtue of her father's having served in the royal government of the colony. Thus, tories and patriots mingled freely at the ball.

One of the Tories, a sixteen-year-old girl named Elizabeth De Blois, caught the eye of the dashing general, and he immediately laid siege to her, despite his assignment to raise troops.

When Arnold's initial advances had no effect on her, he managed to obtain a large supply of European silks, despite the fact that America was virtually blockaded by the British fleet. Arnold had these gorgeous materials made into dresses and delivered a trunkful of them to the lovely Betsy, along with an ardent note proclaiming his worship. Unfortunately for Arnold, Betsy never answered his letter, and merely sent the trunk of dresses back.

Shortly after this setback, Arnold was hit with the first of a series of senseless congressional rebuffs. By the established military custom of seniority, Arnold was the next ranking brigadier general to be promoted to major general. But Congress decided that seniority alone was a dangerous criterion for promotion, since it established an internal army power which, Congress felt, thwarted the civilian government. So the legislators in Philadelphia compromised by promoting five brigadiers to major general, based on a per-state quota and also on how many troops each state had sent to the Continental army.

Those brigadiers promoted over Arnold's head were William Alexander of New Jersey (who claimed the title

Lord Stirling, and was thus addressed by his troops);
Thomas Mifflin and Arthur St. Clair of Pennsylvania;
Adam Stephen of Virginia; and Benjamin Lincoln of
Massachusetts—all grossly inferior to Benedict Arnold as
military leaders.

To soften the impact on his impetuous friend, Washington wrote Arnold a letter explaining what had happened.

We have lately had several promotions to the rank of
major general and I am at a loss whether you have had a
preceding appointment, as the newspapers announce, or
whether you have been omitted through some mistake. Should
the latter be the case, I beg you will not take any hasty steps
in consequence of it; but allow time for recollection, which,
I flatter myself, will remedy any error that may have been
made. My endeavors to that end shall not be wanting.

True to his word, Washington immediately wrote to
his fellow Virginian in Congress Richard Henry Lee, in-
quiring whether

. . . General Arnold's non-promotion was owing to accident
or design; and the cause of it. Surely a more active, a more
spirited and sensible officer, fills no department in your army.
Not seeing him then in the list of major generals, and no mention being made of him, has given me uneasiness, as it is not
to be presumed (being the oldest brigadier) that he will continue in service under such a slight.

Congress had made Arnold look like a fool, and Washington, who recognized Arnold's value to the Continental
army, was doing everything possible to keep his mercurial
subordinate from resigning his commission over such a
dispute.

From Arnold's point of view, considering his previous
relations with civilian governing bodies, the episode constituted a public disgrace. In his eyes, as he wrote to Washington, Congress's action was

. . . a very civil way of requesting my resignation as unqualified for the office I hold. My commission was conferred unsolicited, and received with pleasure only as a means of serving my country. With equal pleasure I resign it when I can no longer serve my country with honor. The person who, void of nice feelings of honor, will tamely condescend to give up his right and retain a commission at the exense of his reputation, I hold as a disgrace to the army and unworthy of the glorious cause in which we are engaged.

We can see the man, bristling with baffled rage, trying to compose a letter to Washington that was respectful and friendly but also full of the frustration and wrath that were consuming him. Accustomed to writing concisely and swiftly—often with the British army breathing down his neck—Arnold now had to write carefully.

And in this letter we get the first whiff of self-righteousness that was to become stronger and stronger over the years as his bitterness increased. Like many an ambitious man, Arnold often was challenged and questioned about his motives, and in justifying them to others he rapidly convinced himself.

When I entered the service of my country [Arnold continued], my character was unimpeached. I have sacrificed my interest, ease, and happiness in her cause. It is rather a misfortune than a fault that my exertions have not been crowned with success. I am conscious of the rectitude of my intentions.

In justice therefore, to my own character and for the satisfaction of my friends, I must request a court of inquiry into my conduct . . .

In a letter dated April 3, 1777, Washington shows a delicate balance of sympathy toward Arnold and loyalty to Congress. He started by explaining the reasoning of Congress: ". . . as Connecticut had already two major generals, it was their full share. I confess that this is a strange mode of reasoning, but it may serve to show you that the promotion which was due to your seniority was not overlooked for want of merit in you."

As for Arnold's threatened resignation if Congress had indeed passed him over, Washington told him:

The point does not now admit of a doubt, and is of so delicate a nature that I will not even undertake to advise; your own feelings must be your guide.

As no particular charge is alleged against you, I do not see upon what ground you can demand a board of inquiry. Besides, public bodies are not amenable for their actions; they place and displace at pleasure and all the satisfaction that an individual can obtain when he is overlooked is, if innocent, a consciousness that he has not deserved such treatment for his honest exertions.

Your determination not to quit your present command while any danger to the public might ensue from your leaving it, deserves my thanks and justly entitles you to the thanks of your country.

Arnold could read only one message in this letter. Washington expected him to resign in order to preserve his honor. Not to resign would be an admission that perhaps Congress was justified in its action. But for Arnold to resign was asking the man voluntarily to forgo that which he loved best. The excitement of leading men into battle, the crackle of musketry and the roar of the cannon, overcoming impossible odds, and outfighting the most powerful, polished army in the world—all these were Arnold's sustenance, the fuel on which his incredible energy ran.

Arnold returned to New Haven, uncertain of what to do but knowing that ultimately he must resign. Once again, an unexpected call to action solved Arnold's dilemma. On April 25, 1777, the British landed 2,000 troops under the command of the British Royal Governor of New York, William Tryon, at Compo Point, near Norwalk,

Connecticut. The British troops marched to Danbury, where they destroyed everything they could get their hands on. What was left over was put to the torch.

Arnold was awakened in his New Haven home by a messenger, telling him of the landing of the British troops. Jumping out of bed and into his uniform, Arnold spurred his horse through a driving rain, with mud flying around him. He picked up General Wooster at Redding, and volunteers and militiamen joined them in their gallop toward Danbury. At Bethel, four miles from Danbury, they could see the glow of the blazing city. They also learned that Tryon intended to march back to his ships immediately, obviously satisfied with giving the rebels a little taste of real warfare.

Arnold and Wooster sized up their forces and realized that some 700 untrained farmers and militiamen could not hope to successfully attack an enemy force of 2,000 experienced soldiers. So Arnold took 500 men to Ridgefield, while Wooster took 200. Arnold was to erect a barricade and force an encounter with the British while Wooster was to fall on the British from behind, driving the lobster-coats between the two American forces.

Arnold placed 200 men behind the barricade, and spread the other 300 out along either flank. When the British arrived and started pounding the barricade with grapeshot, Arnold rode up and down the lines behind the barricade, shouting encouragement and telling the men to hold their fire until the British were almost on top of them. The fire continued on both sides for several minutes, until the British succeeded in outflanking Arnold by gaining control of a hill overlooking his left. When the troops saw this, they began to retreat. Arnold, as usual, was the last to leave, and this nearly cost him his life. A troop of advancing Britishers spotted him, took aim, and fired. His horse fell instantly, riddled by bullets. Arnold was unharmed, but one of his feet was caught in the stirrup. He was hacking away at the leather with his sword when a soldier, waving his bayonet, ran toward him, shouting, "Surrender! You are my prisoner!"

"Not yet!" Arnold shouted, pulling out his loaded pistol and firing it point-blank at the British soldier, killing him instantly. Arnold escaped, obtained a new horse, and immediately set about reorganizing his forces. General Wooster had been killed earlier during an attack on the British.

The British camped that night near Ridgefield, and Arnold spent the night trying to rally his men and obtain fresh recruits to harass the enemy as it marched back to the ships in the same style that American militia had sniped away at the British on their retreat from Concord to Boston at the very start of the war.

The American harassment slowed the British but did not prevent them from reaching the beach. Within minutes, the British landed a fresh force of marines to repulse the rebels. When Arnold tried to lead a charge against the British, he found himself galloping alone. Turning his head from the blazing musketry and cannon, Arnold pleaded with his men to join him, but they wouldn't.

A bullet tore through his coat, and his second horse was wounded, but Arnold once again escaped death or capture. The British successfully returned to their ships, but they suffered many times the casualties of the Americans.

This insignificant skirmish of the Revolution was important to Benedict Arnold, for the accounts of his bravery and daring rang throughout the colonies and even in the halls of Congress. The politicians, yielding at last to Arnold's increasing popularity, promoted him to major general on May 2, but they did not restore his seniority over the five who had been promoted over him. Both Washington and Arnold were dumfounded by Congress's behavior and, with Washington's blessing, Arnold rode south to Philadelphia to obtain satisfaction. Washington wrote to Congress about Arnold's complaints:

These considerations are not without weight, though I pretend not to judge what motives may have influenced the conduct of Congress on this occasion. It is needless to say anything of this gentleman's military character. It is universally known that he has always distinguished himself as a judicious, brave officer of great activity, enterprise and perseverance.

Arnold's old nemesis, John Brown, had been busy in his one-man vendetta and, after resigning in disgust from the army when he could not obtain Arnold's court-martial, he printed up the series of wild, unfounded charges he had made previously against Arnold.

Arnold sent a letter to Congress on May 20, enclosing a copy of Brown's charges, and expressed his unhappiness

. . . to find that having made every sacrifice of fortune, ease and domestic happiness to serve my country, I am publicly impeached (in particular by Lt.-Col. Brown) of a catalogue of crimes which, if true, ought to subject me to disgrace, infamy and the just resentment of my countrymen. Conscious of the rectitude of my intentions, however I may have erred in judgement, I must request the favor of Congress to point out some mode by which my conduct, and that of my accusers, may be inquired into and justice done to the innocent and injured.

His reference to errors in judgment was probably just a polite phrase to cover any petty accusations.

Congress took one look at Arnold's letter and Brown's accusations, and immediately voted

That the quartermaster general be directed to procure a horse and present the same, properly caparisoned, to Major General Arnold, in the name of this Congress as a token of their approbation of his gallant conduct in the action against the enemy in their late enterprise to Danbury, in which General Arnold had one horse killed under him and another wounded.

In almost the same breath, Congress referred Brown's accusations to the Board of War, for investigation and a report. The board interviewed Arnold and reported that it was satisfied that Arnold had behaved properly and praised his conduct, "so cruelly and groundlessly aspersed in the publication" issued by Brown. Congress accepted the board's report but failed to return Arnold's seniority or to act on his expense account for the Canadian invasion.

As in the Ticonderoga campaign, Arnold did not keep precise records while fighting in Canada. Instead, he took from his own pocket whatever monies were needed, assuming that Congress would reimburse him. Once again, the man of action was too busy fighting to bother with accounts.

What Arnold's sessions with the congressional committee amounted to was that Congress was not about to pay out a large sum of money unless Arnold could prove he had spent it. Instead, Congress offered more than what Arnold could prove but less than he actually claimed. But Benedict Arnold was not a man to compromise over a matter of principle, and spending his own money was very

much a matter of principle. He would not settle for anything less than he claimed he had spent, and to accept anything less would be a direct affront to his honor. The more
Arnold made of the issue, the more important it seemed
to him, and the more his sense of self-righteousness increased. His favorite phrase in his letters was "conscious of
my own rectitude."

After months of haggling and dickering, Arnold was a
deeply frustrated man. The money was one thing, but his
seniority was equally important, and Congress's continued
refusal to restore it to him drove him finally, on July 11,
to submit his resignation to Congress, along with the
proviso that should his country need him and were his
proper rank restored, he would gladly lay down his life for
his country.

While Arnold was in the deepest depression of his life,
an emergency letter from Washington was being carried
by courier to Congress. It reported that the British forces
Arnold had held at bay the previous autumn were now
moving unrestricted over Lake Champlain under the command of Burgoyne. They had seized Ticonderoga and had
marched inland to capture Fort Ann. The British plan to
split the colonies seemed on the verge of success.

Upon this occasion [Washington wrote hurriedly], I
would take the liberty to suggest to Congress the propriety
of sending an active, spirited officer to conduct and lead them
on. If General Arnold has settled his affairs and can be spared
from Philadelphia, I would recommend him for the business
and that he should immediately set out for the Northern department. He is active, judicious and brave, and an officer in
whom the militia will repose the greatest confidence. Besides
this, he is well-acquainted with that country and with the
routes and most important passes and defiles in it. I do not
think he can render more signal services or be more usefully

employed at this time than in this way. I am persuaded his presence and activity will animate the militia greatly and spur them on to a becoming conduct; I could wish him to be engaged in a more agreeable service, to be with better troops, but circumstances call for his exertions in this way, and I have no doubt of his adding much to the honors he has already acquired.

Washington's letter, which was dated July 10, 1777, was read to Congress the day before Arnold's. When Arnold's resignation was received, Congress decided to officially ignore it, since Washington's letter had predated it.

Congress had the most warmly praising sections of Washington's letter copied out and sent to Arnold, along with an order that he proceed immediately to the north. No mention was made of his seniority or his unpaid expenses. Arnold knew that to accept such a charge after he had submitted his resignation might forever ruin his case, but he resolved the problem by requesting Congress to suspend action on his resignation until he returned.

After Arnold had galloped off, Congress again refused to grant him his seniority. But not all delegates were hostile toward Arnold. Many of those who voted against him were acting out of what they considered the best interests of the new nation, which had to assert the dominance of the civilian government over the military.

However, at least one delegate, Henry Laurens of South Carolina, was disgusted by the shabby treatment given Arnold, pointing out that Arnold's request had been refused "not because he was deficient in merit or that his demand was not well founded but because he asked for it and that granting at such an instance would be derogatory to the honor of Congress."

5. *The Road to Saratoga*

FOR THE LAST TIME as an American officer, Benedict Arnold saddled his horse and rode north to defend his country. Stopping by Washington's headquarters in the lovely Ford Mansion at Morristown, New Jersey, Arnold was able to personally thank the commander in chief for his unswerving support.

He and Washington discussed the northern crisis in detail, dwelling on the large British force under command of the erstwhile playboy and playwright Burgoyne. Burgoyne had superseded the infinitely more competent Sir Guy Carleton, who remained behind to protect Quebec. Washington was pessimistic, but Arnold immediately began to outline plans to halt the British and turn them back.

Unfortunately for Arnold, he was not in command of the Army of the North and had to accept orders from whoever happened to be in command at the moment, the aristocratic Schuyler or the plebeian Gates. Arnold foresaw no problem here, since he got along equally well with both men. Congress, however, kept seesawing between the two generals, first appointing Gates as commander, then Schuyler, then Gates.

Washington also discussed with Arnold the unpleasant prospect of having to take orders from Arthur St. Clair, one of the five men promoted to major general over

Arnold's head. Both men were convinced that St. Clair was incompetent after the Pennsylvanian lost the supposedly impregnable Fort Ticonderoga to the British with scarcely a shot fired. What neither man knew was that St. Clair had not abandoned the fort out of cowardice or stupidity, but rather because he saw that the British had outfoxed him and were in a superior position. What happened requires a brief digression.

Ticonderoga, or Fort Ti, as the Americans called it, has been mentioned several times in this book as strategically important. It stands near the southern end of Lake Champlain, jutting out from the western shore. A few miles to the southwest, Lake George empties its waters into a narrow gorge, which flows into Lake Champlain near Ticonderoga. Across the lake from the fort stands a small bluff some fifty feet high rather pompously christened Mount Independence by the patriots. The only passageway out of Lake Champlain is between this bluff and the fort, either to the southeast and toward the Hudson or directly into Lake George and south to Albany, the target of the British expedition.

Some two miles northwest of Ticonderoga stands Mount Hope, and about a mile to the southwest is Sugar Loaf Hill, a conical elevation rising 750 feet above the shore.

At the suggestion of the artist-soldier Colonel John Trumbull, whom we last met accompanying Arnold on a trip north, all the hills and mountains within firing range of Ti were fortified. But when Trumbull suggested fortifying Sugar Loaf Hill, closest to the fort, General Gates abruptly refused, claiming that it was inaccessible to both him and the enemy.

British Major General William Phillips, second-in-command and a crack artillerist, did not share Gates's pessimism.

"Where a goat can go a man can go, and where a man can go he can drag a gun," Phillips remarked dryly, and called on his engineers to open a road to the top. Work started on July 4, and on the morning of July 5, St. Clair spotted men and cannon atop Sugar Loaf, at a comfortable firing distance of 1,400 yards.

St. Clair saw that Ticonderoga could no longer be defended, and he called a council of war which unanimously agreed that the fort should be abandoned that night. St. Clair was no genius, but he was not the coward or fool that his colleagues made him out to be. Born in Scotland, he had served in the British army during the French and Indian War and had participated in the siege of Louisburg and the dramatic British capture of Quebec. After the war, he married an American and settled with her in Pennsylvania. When the Revolution came, he joined the rebel army.

St. Clair was simply one of the first victims of Horatio Gates's capacity to make mistakes and then stick by them in the face of all criticism. Gates—not St. Clair—had said no to fortifying Sugar Loaf, even though Trumbull, Anthony Wayne, and the limping Benedict Arnold climbed the most difficult side, the steep eastern wall, all the way to the top. Horatio Gates was one of those men who do not like to admit error or misjudgment. All of this weighed heavily on Arnold when he reached the northern army at Fort Edward in late July.

To those who participated in the Revolution, the pragmatic question was: who would win? True, a handful of Americans laid their money on the rebel cause and stuck

out their necks, but the majority of Americans were willing to see which side was the stronger before deciding.
This attitude was not helpful for the army enlisters and the
professional patriots who daily encouraged other men to
go out and fight to preserve the freedom and well-being of
the politicians and bureaucrats.

The morale of the army that Arnold found huddled at
Fort Edward was abysmally low. Burgoyne's sweep down
Lake Champlain and his effortless capture of Ticonderoga
had unnerved the Continental troops.

A story circulating among the Continental army concerned the final American involvement at Ticonderoga.
After St. Clair had evacuated the fort, he had left one
battery of field artillery to fire a final salvo at the British
and then retreat. The British, under command of General
Simon Fraser, approached the battery carefully. To their
astonishment, then amusement, the British attackers found
all four American gunners sprawled in a drunken stupor
beside a cask of Madeira.

Another surprise was in store for Arnold. At Fort
Edward he learned that Colonel Barry St. Leger was swing-
ing in from the west with more than 2,000 British troops,
Tory regiments and fierce Indians under the leadership of
the British-educated Chief Joseph Brant. This force fol-
lowed the Mohawk River toward its confluence with the
Hudson and, on August 3, laid siege to Fort Stanwix in
New York State. In an abortive attempt to relieve the siege,
Americans engaged British troops at the bloody Battle of
Oriskany and were soundly trounced. The British then
resumed their siege of Fort Stanwix.

Meanwhile, the British had inadvertently aroused deep

American resentment by their failure to punish the two Indian guides who had accompanied pretty young Jane McCrea as she was traveling to join her Tory fiancé in Burgoyne's company. Fighting over her, the two Indians killed and then scalped Jane. Burgoyne, when he heard this story, was revolted and ordered the capture and execution of the murderers. But his aides pointed out that such action would alienate Britain's valuable Indian allies. Burgoyne was a humane man, disgusted with this act of barbarity, and he knew that his failure to avenge the murder of the young American would hurt his cause. On learning of the Jane McCrea atrocity, Gates immediately fired off an outraged dispatch to Burgoyne, who returned the following account:

> In regard to Miss McCrea, her fate wanted not of the tragic display you have labored to give it to make it as sincerely abhorred and lamented by me as it can be by the tenderest of her friends. . . . Upon the first intelligence of this event I obliged the Indians to deliver the murderer into my hands; and tho to have punished him by our laws or principles of justice would have been perhaps unprecedented, he certainly should have suffered an ignominious death had I not been convinced by circumstances and observation, beyond the possibility of a doubt, that a pardon, under the forms which I prescribed and they accepted, would be more efficacious than an execution to prevent similar mischiefs.

Schuyler, who wasn't sure from day to day whether he or Gates commanded the Army of the North, knew that he had to send a force to relieve the siege of Fort Stanwix. He called for volunteers among his brigadiers, and the silence was frightening. Then a raspy voice was heard. "I'll take it!"

It was not a brigadier but a major general, the second-

in-command of the Army of the North, Benedict Arnold.
Schuyler was delighted and immediately issued orders.

Starting out in mid-August, 1777, with less than a
thousand men, Arnold knew that he would have to recruit
volunteers on the way if he was to be any match for St.
Leger's superior force.

While trying to decide how best to attack St. Leger,
whose troops were closing in on Fort Stanwix, in the
classical siege method of digging zigzag trenches, Arnold
learned that a British foraging party under the command
of Colonel Baum had been slaughtered by American forces
commanded by General John Stark near Bennington, Vermont, the first of Burgoyne's major setbacks. Arnold was
also informed by messenger that the new commander of
the Army of the North was his old friend, Horatio Gates.

Arnold was pacing back and forth in his field headquarters, wondering how he could rout St. Leger's superior
force, when the solution suddenly presented itself in the
form of a half-wit. Hon Yost Schuyler, distantly related
to General Schuyler and a member of a Tory family, had
been arrested by American troops and condemned to be
hanged as a spy. Arnold discovered that Hon Yost was well
known among the Indians, who considered idiots the special
favorites of the gods (a not unusual concept, for medieval
European Christians often shared the same view).

Arnold knew exactly what he must do. Summoning
Hon Yost and his family to his quarters, Arnold solemnly
told the half-wit to prepare for death. After listening for a
few moments to the outbursts of his family, Arnold offered
to spare Hon Yost's life on condition that he travel to the
British camp and inform the superstitious Indians in St.
Leger's army that the fearsome Benedict Arnold was advancing with overwhelming forces.

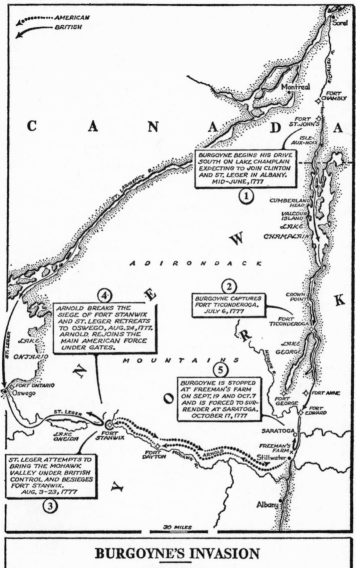

AMERICAN
BRITISH

CANADA

Sorel

Montreal

FORT
CHAMBLY

FORT
ST. JOHN'S

ISLE
AUX-NOIX

ST. LAWRENCE R.

BURGOYNE BEGINS HIS DRIVE
SOUTH ON LAKE CHAMPLAIN
EXPECTING TO JOIN CLINTON
AND ST. LEGER IN ALBANY.
MID-JUNE, 1777
①

CUMBERLAND
HEAD

VALCOUR
ISLAND

LAKE
CHAMPLAIN

N E W

A D I R O N D A C K

Y O R K

④
ARNOLD BREAKS THE
SIEGE OF FORT STANWIX
AND ST. LEGER RETREATS
TO OSWEGO, AUG.24,1777.
ARNOLD REJOINS THE
MAIN AMERICAN FORCE
UNDER GATES.

②
BURGOYNE CAPTURES
FORT TICONDEROGA.
JULY 6, 1777

CROWN
POINT

FORT
TICONDEROGA

ST. LEGER

LAKE
ONTARIO

M O U N T A I N S

LAKE
GEORGE

HUDSON R.

FORT ONTARIO
Oswego

⑤
BURGOYNE IS STOPPED
AT FREEMAN'S FARM
ON SEPT. 19 AND OCT.7
AND IS FORCED TO SUR-
RENDER AT SARATOGA.
OCTOBER 17, 1777

FORT
GEORGE

FORT ANNE

FORT
EDWARD

ST. LEGER

LAKE
ONEIDA

FORT
STANWIX

SARATOGA

FREEMAN'S
FARM

FORT
DAYTON

MOHAWK R.

ARNOLD

Stillwater

③
ST. LEGER ATTEMPTS TO
BRING THE MOHAWK
VALLEY UNDER BRITISH
CONTROL AND BESIEGES
FORT STANWIX.
AUG. 3-23, 1777

Albany

30 MILES

BURGOYNE'S INVASION

JUNE—OCTOBER
1777

Hon Yost may indeed have been an idiot, but he was clever enough to expand on Arnold's basic idea by suggesting that the Americans riddle his coat with bullet holes to make his story of a narrow escape more convincing.

The Indians accompanying St. Leger's expedition had been promised that they were along primarily to make the army look larger, and that they wouldn't have to do much fighting. At Oriskany, however, the Indians were in the thick of the fight. Now St. Leger, who had learned of Arnold's march, instructed the Indians to ambush the smaller American force.

The Indians who knew Arnold as the "Dark Eagle," the name given him by the Abenaki chief, Natanis, knew that he was a fighter who would not easily be ambushed. They held a powwow and were debating what to do when Hon Yost burst from the forest, running and screaming that Arnold was coming. Although they had reverential respect for the childlike Hon Yost, the Indians wanted to know how many men were accompanying Arnold. He simply pointed up to the leaves on the trees.

In terror, the Indians hustled Hon Yost into the headquarters of St. Leger, and he repeated his story of being pursued by the Americans who, with Arnold at their head, were two thousand strong. An Oneida Indian, sent by Arnold to follow Hon Yost and see that he said what he was supposed to say, recruited a few friends and brought them into St. Leger's camp. They repeated Hon Yost's story and embellished it with even more frightening details.

According to Dr. James Thacher, surgeon in the Continental army:

This stratagem was successful: the Indians instantly determined to quit their ground and make their escape, nor was it in the power of St. Leger and Sir John Johnson with all their art of persuasion to prevent it. When St. Leger remonstrated with them, the reply of the chiefs was, "When we marched down you told us there would be no fighting for us Indians: we might go down and smoke our pipes, but now a number of our warriors have been killed and you mean to sacrifice us." The consequence was that St. Leger, finding himself deserted by his Indians, to the number of seven or eight hundred, deemed his situation so hazardous that he decamped in the greatest hurry and confusion, leaving his tents with most of his artillery and stores in the field. General Arnold with his detachment was now at liberty to return to the main army at Stillwater; and thus we have clipped the right wing of Burgoyne.

When he arrived at Fort Stanwix, which was no longer under siege, Arnold naturally listened eagerly to the many voices telling him that his name alone had caused the rout of the British. This was heady praise indeed. Arnold rode back to the American camp knowing that his very name was enough to strike fear into the hearts of British, Indians, and loyalists. Yet as he turned back toward Albany, he was entering a hornet's nest of intrigue and political savagery for which he was ill prepared.

Arnold had effectively cleared the British from the Mohawk Valley, and the defeat of the Hessians at Bennington had seriously crippled Burgoyne. With winter rapidly approaching, the dapper British general had to decide immediately either to return to Canada or to push on to Albany. The British army could not bivouac in the wilderness; it required a major town like Albany.

But to push toward Albany would mean that Burgoyne would have to cross to the west bank of the Hudson and sever both his supply trains and his channels of communication with Canada. Realizing that he was not going

to get the help he expected from General William Howe
in New York, Burgoyne decided that he could not retreat
after coming this far. Therefore, he made the only possible
decision and, on September 15, crossed the Hudson with
thirty days' worth of supplies.

Arnold, having arrived in Albany flushed with his
continuing success, found out for sure that his commander
was now Horatio Gates, and the two old friends greeted
one another warmly. Gates appointed Arnold to command
his left wing and ordered him north with Colonel Thaddeus Kosciusko to select and fortify an impregnable position commanding the river road leading south to Albany,
along which Burgoyne's troops would have to march.
Arnold and the Polish engineer decided that the high rise
of land south of Stillwater, known as Bemis Heights after
a man named Bemis who operated a tavern there, would be
ideal, and it was heavily fortified. In Arnold's view, the
position would enable the Americans to fight from the
woods and hills in the guerrilla-style warfare they had
perfected, and it would also keep Burgoyne's troops off
balance by denying them the open-field, hand-to-hand
fighting that was the traditional European way of doing
battle.

While Arnold's plans for the coming engagement with
Burgoyne were premised on the new style of warfare,
Gates was thinking along more conventional lines. Burgoyne's army was decimated and short of provisions.
Burgoyne would have to lay siege to the American stronghold on Bemis Heights, and after a brief period the British
would starve themselves to the point of surrender.

There is something to be said for both arguments, and
Gates was not nearly the incompetent that some historians

have made him out to be. He was a good administrator but conservative in his ideas of warfare. He did not think that a general's place was at the head of his troops, but, rather, back at headquarters, coordinating the battle.

To Gates, it was better to draw the enemy slowly along until it fell, whereas Arnold knew that the British army was unequaled in siegework and could possibly drive the Americans out of Bemis Heights. Arnold felt that militarily the soundest move was a lightning attack on an exposed flank.

This difference between the two men on military strategy was not the only one to begin to surface. Gates remembered ordering Arnold to conduct a defensive action against the British on Lake Champlain the previous year, but Arnold had disregarded his instructions and had bravely engaged in an all-out battle in which he lost nearly his entire fleet.

Gates also noticed that Arnold was filling his staff with former aides to the hated Schuyler, and Gates was particularly insulted when Arnold picked as his secretary the twenty-four-year-oid Lieutenant Colonel Richard Varick, an outspoken friend of Schuyler's who had quarreled publicly with Gates.

Thus, when news came to Gates's headquarters in the little red wooden house atop Bemis Heights that the British were moving in three columns toward Freeman's Farm, Gates restrained Arnold from galloping off to immediate battle. He wanted his hotheaded subordinate where he could keep an eye on him. But at Arnold's insistence, Gates agreed to send out Dan Morgan's riflemen and some light infantry regiments under the command of Henry Dearborn to engage Burgoyne's column, which had arrived at the deserted Freeman log cabin, set in the middle of an open field.

The date was September 19, 1777, and autumn was already moving through the Hudson Valley, changing the green leaves to all shades of scarlet, yellow, and orange.

Morgan and Dearborn discovered the British pickets in Freeman's field and chased them into the woods, where they ran into the force of Burgoyne's army. The Americans retreated to their own forest while Burgoyne ordered his men to take up battle positions in the field. During their retreat into the forest, Morgan's men became scattered, but his imitation of a turkey call reunited the divided command.

The tide of fighting at what was to become known as the Battle of Freeman's Farm, the first engagement of the two-part Battle of Saratoga (named for the nearby town), swayed back and forth.

Arnold had been standing with Gates outside the general headquarters as couriers galloped to a stop, shouted their news, then returned to the battle front. What precisely happened between the two men is not clear, for the only on-the-spot recorder was Gates's secretary, Colonel James Wilkinson, one of the most devious men in American history. Since his is the only account, it must be given some recognition. According to Wilkinson, Arnold continued to plead with Gates to let him take charge of the American field forces, but Gates was adamant in insisting that Arnold remain by his side. He did not want another Valcour Island disaster.

Finally, when a messenger reported the battle to be a stalemate, Arnold raced for his horse, shouting, "By God, I will soon put an end to it!"

Before Gates could open his mouth, Arnold was a cloud of dust as he spurred his horse toward the sound of the muskets and cannon. Gates recovered his senses long enough to send Wilkinson after Arnold to order him back to camp. Wilkinson succeeded in overtaking Arnold, who was furious but obedient to Gates's direct order.

The two men met in an explosion of temper. Arnold felt thwarted because Gates had prevented him from leading what could have been the decisive charge against the British, and Gates by now was in ill humor over his subordinate's rashness. The fact that the Americans had to withdraw at sunset, leaving the British in possession of the field, furthered Arnold's fury, and his resentment was carefully fueled by members of his staff who had served under Schuyler and who hated Gates. At the same time, Gates was being primed with anti-Arnold sentiments by Wilkinson and others on his staff who were jealous or resentful of Arnold's reputation and talents.

Until very recently, American historians placed Arnold at the head of the troops at the Battle of Freeman's Farm, but the evidence to the contrary is strong. There seems little doubt that Arnold did indeed attempt to join the battle and that he was called back by Gates's order. The behavior of the two men during the days that passed before the decisive Battle of Bemis Heights, in which Arnold smashed the British force in complete defiance of Gates's orders, was increasingly hostile.

When Arnold complained that Gates was hamstringing him, Gates purred nastily that as far as he knew, Arnold had resigned his commission to Congress and had no right to demand a command. When Arnold bridled at the insult, Gates told him that Arnold would shortly be replaced by fat old General Benjamin Lincoln, the Massachusetts militia commander who had been promoted over Arnold's head.

And if Arnold didn't like the way Gates was running the war, why, Arnold was at liberty to leave any time he wished, in order to present his case to General Washington and Congress. Both Gates and Arnold knew that such a departure was unthinkable, especially now that Burgoyne was about to fall into American hands.

In a series of actions seemingly calculated to drive Arnold to physical violence, Gates coolly detached Morgan's riflemen and all other regiments from Arnold's command, leaving him impotent as a general. Gates also, in his description of the first battle to Congress, made no mention of Arnold, even though the regiments which fought were all under Arnold's command.

The two men met frequently and stormily in Gates's headquarters atop Bemis Heights. Charges and counter-charges flew, insults were exchanged, and the voices of the men rose to screaming pitch, often climaxed by Arnold's slamming the door as he stalked back to his camp.

Arnold knew he was a better leader than Gates and that he could win a smashing victory against Burgoyne. Gates, who had lobbied and persuaded his way into this important command, knew his strategy and was not about to have the laurels of victory seized by his gifted, impetuous lieutenant.

Arnold finally announced that he would leave to join Washington, where perhaps he might be permitted to use his abilities in a better capacity than at Bemis Heights. Word of Arnold's decision spread rapidly through the American camp, and several officers, led by New Hampshire's General Enoch Poore—no friend of Arnold's—circulated a petition among the general officers that Arnold reconsider his decision and remain where he could do the American cause the most good. Every general officer except General Lincoln—and, of course, Gates—signed it, and Arnold agreed to swallow his pride and not desert the army that needed him so badly.

By now completely stripped of his command, Arnold could only pace around his camp, boiling as he saw lesser officers hurrying into Gates's headquarters for strategy meetings. Arnold knew that Burgoyne had taken advantage of the American withdrawal from Freeman's Farm to erect redoubts on the slight elevations, to function as bastions from which his troops could move out for a last determined effort to defeat Gates and gain access to the river road running to Albany. Burgoyne knew that to march along the road under the cannon surmounting Bemis Heights would be suicidal, so a final attack had to be made to rout the rebels.

Deserters were common to each side in the Revolution, and Burgoyne was fully informed of the controversy between Gates and Arnold. Gates he held in contempt, but Arnold was another matter. As Carleton's second-in-command the previous year, the British commander had seen Arnold in battle on Lake Champlain, and knew that the presence of the man who had so rattled the British navy could be disastrous for his hopes. Burgoyne decided that it was time to strike, basing his decision on the fact that his army had only a few days' provisions left, and it was either strike or starve.

Burgoyne started to move out on the morning of October 7 to force a conflict, and by noon the Americans were preparing to greet him appropriately. Benedict Arnold, standing in front of his tent within sight of Gates's headquarters, heard the cannon and the muskets, and he watched as messengers rode up and then back to the lines.

Arnold mounted his horse in time to see streams of wounded Americans being carried back to the field hospital. The smell of powder filled the air. Then something snapped in Benedict Arnold.

Some say he was drunk. Others claim he had been taking opium. But given Arnold's impetuous nature and previous outbursts of temper, we may conclude that he simply reached the end of his patience. Drawing his sword, he shouted, "No man will keep me in my tent this day!" and rode off furiously to join the action.

Gates saw him go, and once again he ordered an aide, Major John Armstrong, to overtake Arnold and bring him back to headquarters.

But this time no man or horse could stop Benedict Arnold. He knew that Gates would be sending someone after him, so he spurred his horse mercilessly.

The rest of the battle has already been described. Arnold took personal command of several floundering regiments and led them against the Balcarres redoubt. When this failed to fall, he galloped to the left and led a succesful charge through the sally port of the Breymann redoubt, which was on higher ground than the Balcarres redoubt, thus permitting its cannon to be trained on the other by American artillerymen.

This gallop was Arnold's last and greatest. It is useless to speculate on what might have happened had Arnold left the northern army and rejoined Washington. He might have become the supreme general in the Revolution, but

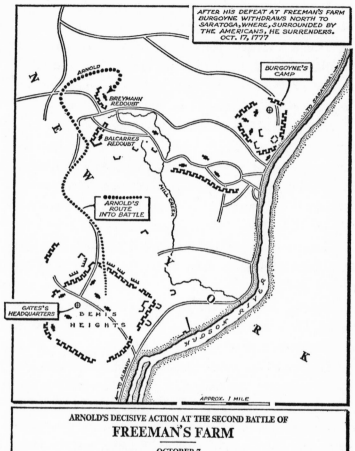

ARNOLD'S DECISIVE ACTION AT THE SECOND BATTLE OF

FREEMAN'S FARM

OCTOBER 7
1777

Gates could have lost the battle. Gates's conservative old-world strategy was not entirely without logic, but had he holed up on Bemis Heights, the British might well have found a way to slip through to Albany. Had this happened, the American cause would have been seriously compromised, for the capture of Albany would have been a moral victory for the British and would most certainly have brought Sir Henry Clinton, who succeeded Howe as British commander, up the Hudson with enough troops to cut the colonies in half.

On the other hand, had Arnold returned to serve directly under Washington, he would have received command of the left wing of the army and who knows what miracles he might have worked.

Instead, he merely won the Battle of Saratoga almost singlehanded, a victory that the American Ambassador to France, Benjamin Franklin, was able to use as the final argument to obtain complete and open support of the rebel cause.

Arnold should have been killed at Saratoga. He galloped across a deadly fire of muskets and grapeshot, and he wasn't wounded until after he had led his forces into the Breymann redoubt and victory was certain.

Horatio Gates, of course, received credit for the victory when Burgoyne surrendered several days later in a field outside Stillwater. Arnold was in the hospital, recovering from his leg wound, as he heard the fifes and drums of the defeated British as they marched to lay down their arms.

Enough officers and enlisted men knew of Arnold's contribution to the victory to oblige Gates to make a passing reference to the "gallant General Arnold" in his report to Congress. However, unofficial reports filtering back to Congress and Washington made it clear who had been the victor of Saratoga. The politicians in Philadelphia recognized what an incredible field officer Arnold was, and finally voted to restore his seniority.

But it was too late.

While Arnold lay in his cot in excruciating pain, listening to the celebrations of his men, he was also thinking. Who was this Congress that could arbitrarily pass him over for promotion, then give him the rank of major general without restoring his seniority? After all he had sacrificed, including his own money, his reputation, and his life, how dare the civilian government treat him so shabbily! And it was this same civilian government which named Gates to lead the Army of the North. Where was Gates when the Americans stormed Quebec in a snowstorm? Where was Gates when Arnold led his fleet past the British in a dense fog on Lake Champlain, only to fight a hopeless but delaying battle which discouraged the British from pushing onward that year?

Arnold's thoughts were bitter; no matter how great his past achievements and glories, he had to fight for every shred of official recognition. Bitterness leads to self-pity, which in turn can lead to either withdrawal or retaliation. Arnold was not the man to withdraw from the army or from public life. Revenge did not make much sense unless it brought satisfaction with it.

The more Arnold brooded, the angrier he became. Much of this energy he poured into letters to his friends, to Washington, to Congress, and to anyone he felt like writing.

He knew that he had more than proved himself in

battle and that Washington would recognize his accomplishments and reward him with an appropriate appointment as soon as he was able to move around. But it is just possible that Benedict Arnold was no longer thrilled at the prospect of such honors and recognition. Perhaps the ultimate insult had already been delivered.

PART TWO

6. John André

UNLIKE BENEDICT ARNOLD, John André's rise to fame in the American Revolution came only after years of dreariness in subordinate roles. Captured in November of 1775 by Montgomery's forces at St. John's, Lieutenant André and his fellow officers and soldiers were led off into captivity by the ragtag rebel army they so heartily despised.

There is a charming story told—charming stories abound concerning the ill-fated young André—about his march to internment in Pennsylvania. During the howling winter of 1775–76, André and his fellow British officers were herded into an inn near Lake George, which was already crowded with sleepers. André is said to have bedded down with a portly gentleman who, when the storm kept them both awake, initiated a conversation that lasted through the night.

Upon awakening and donning uniforms, the two bedmates discovered that they belonged to opposing armies. With old-world courtesy, each introduced himself. André's bedmate had been the former Boston bookseller-turned-artillerist, Colonel Henry Knox, on his way to bring the cannon captured from Ticonderoga to Washington's army besieging Boston. The two men parted cordially, destined to meet again in the Dutch Reformed Church of Tappan on a sunny autumn morning in 1780, when General Henry Knox would sit in judgment on Major John André.

The son of a Swiss merchant and a Parisian beauty—who met, married, and settled in England—John André was born in London on May 2 of either 1750 or 1751, depending on whose statistics and records one accepts. Anxious to avoid the business on which his family's fortune was dependent young John André was sent to the University of Geneva, where he studied mathematics and military drawing, with the obvious intention of becoming a professional soldier.

When his father died in 1769, John André suddenly discovered that he would be financially independent for the rest of his life. It was while mourning the death of Anthony André that his family visited the baths in Buxton, and there the young André met Anna Seward, six years his senior, a poet, and an inspiration to him, whom he promptly rechristened "Julia." Always in the company of Julia was Honora Sneyd, the ward of the Seward family, a wilting, silent girl to whom André eventually proposed and who accepted him. During this entire time, young John was virtually chained to the countinghouse, learning his father's business from the bottom up—a prospect he hated.

Then the engagement with Honora fell through, and John André, on January 25, 1771, purchased a commission as second lieutenant in the Royal Welsh Fusiliers. A few months later he bought a first lieutenant's commission in the Seventh Foot of the Royal Fusiliers. Finding peacetime life in London boring, André hied himself to Germany, where he settled down at Göttingen, famed as a military training center. Nine months later, however, he was notified that his regiment was being sent to the American colonies. Instead of sailing directly to Quebec, where his regiment was stationed, André decided to take the "grand tour" of the American colonies first, starting in that most European of cities in the New World, Philadelphia, and progressing northward through noisy New York and seething Boston. Instead of sailing up the Atlantic coast for Quebec, André chose the more scenic route up the Hudson and Lake Champlain.

Settling in with the French and British in Canada, André made himself at home until summoned out into the field to practice tiresome wilderness exercises. André had no idea that in a very short time he would be holed up with the British garrison at St. John's, ultimately surrendering to the American forces under General Richard Montgomery, himself an ex-British officer.

André was interned in Lancaster, Pennsylvania, where he and his fellow British prisoners were regarded with contempt, hatred, and fear. André, a talented artist, dabbled in painting to pass the idle hours, and he soon attracted some of the younger Lancastrians as his pupils. James T. Flexner, in *The Traitor and the Spy*, mentions a legend that the young Robert Fulton, later to graduate from painter to inventor, took his first lessons from the captured British lieutenant.

But late in March the Continental authorities decided it would be best to disperse any large gatherings of captive British officers, in order to forestall possible escapes or insurrections. André was ordered to Carlisle, forty miles away from Lancaster and a true frontier town.

Throughout his captivity, André was in constant fear of his life. Originally a peaceful man, he began to harden

as he watched the behavior of the American woodsmen toward captives, and on more than one occasion he and other
officers were openly threatened by the brave American
rabble. This experience was to prove very important in his
later attitude toward the rebels.

Writing to his relatives about the perils of captivity
among the Americans, André noted:

We were every day pelted and reviled in the streets, and
have been oftentimes invited to smell a brandished hatchet
and reminded of its agreeable effects on the skull, receiving at
the same time promises that we should be murdered the next
day. Several of us have been fired at and we have more than
once been waylaid by men determined to assassinate us, and
escaped by being warned to take different roads. Such is the
brotherly love they in our capitulation promised us.

Had the young lieutenant been held captive in Philadelphia or another civilized center, he might have shared
with General Howe a fondness for the Americans and a
reluctance to shed their blood. However, his captivity was
a daily threat to his life, and he saw the loathsome side of
the rebel character, a side that is not presented in textbook
histories of the Revolution. In short, John André, who was
raised in a civilized society, was subjected to cruelty and
obnoxiousness, and he formed his ideas about warfare in
America accordingly. Unlike Burgoyne, Howe, Clinton,
Lord Germain, Lord North, and King George, André saw
at first hand the low, seamy side of the rebel army, for-
getting that the British army and navy had been augmented
by press gangs operating among the scum of Great Britain.

No other figure in the great Arnold-André conspiracy
had such a taste of the brutality of warfare as had John
André, and he carried that bitterness with him throughout

the Revolution. Dealing with gentlemen as a staff officer in the British army was one thing, but living in daily fear of his life at the hands of the unwashed rabble shook André profoundly. To be spat upon, humiliated, and daily threatened with death is enough to turn the soul of the most forgiving of men.

André was indeed bitter by the time he was exchanged back to the British for American prisoners, and for a brief while he let this bitterness fester. But he was too concerned with his own advancement in the British army to let it color his decisions as he moved from commander to commander.

André and his fellow officers were exchanged in November, 1776, while Washington's army was in full rout across New Jersey from the British, and he promptly made his way back to British headquarters in Manhattan. He immediately came to the attention of Sir William Howe because of the detailed secret maps he had drawn while in captivity. Howe promised the enterprising officer the first available promotion.

Howe was as good as his word, and when André asked permission to purchase a captain's commission, the general gave his blessing. Purchased? Yes indeed.

In the British army commissions were purchased by those who could afford them, which perhaps explains the number of incompetent but highly placed generals in His Majesty's armed forces.

The theory behind the selling of commissions was that this kept the officer corps free of riffraff, since only those of gentle birth or noble means could afford to rise in the army or navy. A soldier with talent but no fortune might rise by his wits to the level of noncommissioned officer or subaltern, but the majority of soldiers and sailors remained at the same level until they were killed, maimed, or too old to fight.

This concept of commissions-for-sale is in sharp contrast to the promotion by seniority or by Congressional whim that prevailed in the Continental army. Promotion by merit was the ideal, and the fact that men such as Benedict Arnold, Nathanael Greene, Daniel Morgan, Anthony Wayne and Henry Knox rose to the top of the army is an indication of the soundness of the American system.

The British had a handful of intelligent officers in America. In addition to André, there was the young Lieutenant Colonel Banastre Tarleton, who dashingly led his cavalry against the rebels in the South, butchering them with a ferocity that made his name synonymous with ruthless bloodshed.

Then there was Sir Guy Carleton, drumming his fingers idly on his desk in Canada while his inept colleagues missed chance after chance to crack the rebellion and restore British rule to the colonies. Sir Guy was just the British general to do that, and he was more than a match for Washington. But politics kept Carleton out of America until after the last guns of Yorktown had stopped firing. Then, for two years, he was in command of the British army in New York while peace negotiations were underway in Paris.

And, finally, there was the man whom André perceived as the ideal British commander, Major General Charles Grey, who arrived at Howe's headquarters in June of 1777. Grey needed an aide, and who was better qualified than the handsome young Captain André, who had made all those marvelous maps of the interior while held prisoner?

Grey and André met and liked one another immediately. Grey could see the simmering bitterness beneath the winning smile of the intelligent young captain. André had obviously ingratiated himself with Howe yet had not been infected with any of Howe's ambivalence toward the American cause.

Howe at heart was a friend of the American cause, and he had been one of the leaders in the Whig party calling for independence. When King George appointed him to crush the rebellion, several Tories smiled sardonically, because they knew that Howe's sense of honor and duty to his King would force him to fight those whose cause he had championed. To Howe's credit, it must be said that he never shirked his duty. Whenever the opportunity presented itself, he attacked the Americans. However, he never concluded a victory by a rout and slaughter of the fleeing rebel troops. He would win the battle, but that was as far as he would go.

General Grey regarded such conduct as befitting a politician-turned-soldier. Grey, on the other hand, was a professional soldier who saw his job as a clear-cut assignment to defeat the enemy by any means whatever. Killing and wounding was part of Grey's whole philosophy of war, and the general who shrinks from killing was regarded as incompetent by Grey.

This is not to say that Charles Grey was the monster that some American histories have painted him. Grey could be jolly and laugh heartily, especially at the witticisms of his new aide-de-camp, Captain André. Grey was good company for his fellow officers and a devoted family man. But when it came to warfare, he was a professional, and he took pride in his work. His sole objective was to decimate and subjugate the enemy, and if he had to kill, wound, and burn to achieve this objective, he would do so without losing a wink of sleep over the horrors of his profession.

John André, a man who considered himself a sensitive poet and a man of letters, allied himself with General Grey and kept a journal of their exploits in the wilds of the colonies.

John André's *Journal* (which can be read in photocopies of the original in several major libraries) is an unusual document. The entries are laconic and brief, no matter how horrible the events he describes.

In July of 1777, Howe at last ordered his troops in New York into transports for a major campaign that was designed to snuff the rebellion with one mighty show of British military superiority. Howe had several options of how to squelch the rebels.

One would be to sail up the Hudson and trap the Continental forces rapidly falling back before the advancing troops of Burgoyne. This was precisely what Howe had been expected to do, according to the plan laid out before the King and Lord Germain by Burgoyne the previous winter. But Germain had neglected to inform Howe of this decision, and Howe reasoned that Burgoyne's army was strong enough to take care of itself. The news that Benedict Arnold was riding north to help lead the retreating Americans impressed Burgoyne, who knew Arnold's capabilities, but not Howe, who had barely heard of the man.

So Howe set sail for the mouth of the Delaware, determined to take Philadelphia, the rebel capital. But the forts guarding the entrance to the river seemed stronger than they actually were, so Howe continued south and sailed up Chesapeake Bay, landing at the Head of Elk.

The march north toward Philadelphia was uneventful, with the exception of a few skirmishes, until the British reached the Brandywine River in southern Pennsylvania. There Washington and his army were waiting for them on the opposite bank of the river. Howe's advance scouts apprised him of the three-mile spread of the American army between Chadd's Ford and Radley Run.

Acting on an elementary military principle—which somehow escaped Washington—Howe sent one column straight for Chadd's Ford under the command of the Hessian General Wilhelm von Knyphausen, while he and Lord Cornwallis took another column on a wide sweep to the left, crossing the river a few miles above the outposts of the Americans. From there, Howe closed in on the rebels' flank while Knyphausen thrust boldly toward the river, only to be driven back by the cannon and troops under General Anthony Wayne. Knyphausen hauled up his cannon and began to batter the rebels, ultimately driving them and their cannon back enough to allow his troops to cross the river.

By now the American forces were retreating rapidly, and one swift blow would have wiped them out. But Howe was content with victory and chose instead to rest his troops and regroup. André, who had little part in this battle, expressed certainty in his letters that Howe could have ended the rebellion with a complete victory at Brandywine. He shared Grey's disgust with Howe's failure to show the rebels what war really is.

Howe was aware of Grey's attitude, so he gave him the distasteful job of wiping out Anthony Wayne's command, which had been picking and sniping at the British as

well as raiding supply wagons on their way to British headquarters.

Grey marched immediately, and by late night of
September 20, 1777, his troops were within striking distance of Wayne's camp near Paoli, Pennsylvania. Grey
ordered his foot soldiers to remove the flints from their
muskets, depriving them of the ability to fire and thus
forcing them to rely on bayonet and musket butt. Captain
André probably checked the various subordinate commanders to make sure that all flints had been removed. The
British moved softly, until they could hear in the distance
the singing, shouting, and music that clearly indicated that
the Americans were having a boisterous party. So much
the better, Grey must have thought. Drunken soldiers have
very slow reflexes. The British moved like panthers, surprising and killing outpost guards. One escaped and ran
back to camp to alert Wayne of the danger. But before
Wayne could do much—he too was pleasantly pickled—
Grey's troops poured into the camp. The men had been
told by Grey that prisoners were a burden to an army, a
broad hint that anyone who took too many rebels alive
might be in trouble.

The British Light Infantry needed no prodding. Composed of the toughest, leanest, nastiest ruffians in His
Majesty's army, the Light Infantry respected commanders
like Grey who refused to coddle the enemy.

Of course, one of the rules of war is that when a man
voluntarily throws down his arms and surrenders, he must
be taken captive as a prisoner of war and treated as a human
being. This was one of the rules that Grey chose to ignore
that night.

GENERAL ARNOLD.

Benedict Arnold, an engraving from the portrait by Du Simitier.
This is the only known portrait taken from life.
Courtesy of the New-York Historical Society, New York City.

Margaret Shippen (Mrs. Benedict Arnold), a pencil drawing
by Major John André. This costume was designed by André.
Yale University Art Gallery.

A self-portrait, by Major John André. André made this pen-and-ink
sketch of himself on the eve of his execution.
Yale University Art Gallery gift of Ebenezer Baldwin BA 1808.

Arnold's march to Quebec. Taken from the journal of Isaac Senter, a military surgeon who accompanied Arnold.
The Metropolitan Museum of Art, bequest of Charles Allen Munn, 1924.

"God Blesse Our Armes," a water color by C. Randle, 1776. This painting, celebrating Arnold's exploits at Valcour Island, shows also the fleet constructed under Arnold's supervision to fight the British on Lake Champlain. *Courtesy Fort Ticonderoga Museum.*

NEW ENGLAND VESSELS at VALCURE BAY — Commander B. ARNOLD — 11 OCTOBRE 1776

Sir Henry Clinton, an engraving by A. H. Ritchie.
*Courtesy of the New-York Historical Society,
New York City.*

At right General John Burgoyne, by Joshua Reynolds.
Copyright the Frick Collection, New York.

West Point as it appeared at the close of the war, by C. Tiebout.
Note the chain across the Hudson to prevent passage of British shipping.
Courtesy of the New-York Historical Society, New York City.

At *right*, André's monument in Westminster Abbey.
Copyright Dean & Chapter of Westminster.

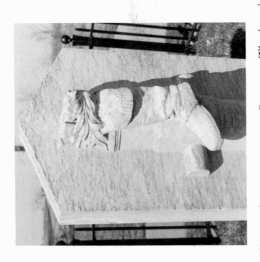

Arnold's nameless monument at Saratoga. The inscription reads: "In memory of the most brilliant soldier of the Continental Army, who was desperately wounded on this spot, the sally port of BURGOYNE'S 'GREAT (WESTERN) REDOUBT' 7th October 1777, winning for his countrymen the decisive battle of the American Revolution and for himself the rank of Major General."

U.S. Department of the Interior National Park Service.

The work was fast, dirty, and brutal. American survivors claimed that men who threw down their arms and surrendered received a bayonet in the belly for their efforts. British troops moved slowly through the campsite, looking for signs of life. The wounded man who did not play dead soon was dead. Bodies were pierced with bayonets, skulls crushed in.

André reports in his *Journal* that some 200 rebels were killed, 40 seriously wounded, and 31 captured. His account very coolly notes that the Light Infantry "put to the bayonet all they came up with and, overtaking the main herd of the fugitives, stabbed great numbers and pressed on their rear till it was thought prudent to order them to desist."

A junior officer called Grey's attention to a large supply of gin left by the now dead Americans, and the officers celebrated their victory with toasts to His Majesty and to the British army. Glasses raised, they drank, laughed, and sang, while around their boots swirled the blood of their victims.

Grey had succeeded in doing what Howe had failed to do for so long—scaring hell out of the Americans. No single British officer brought war closer to home than "No-Flint" Grey, and none would terrorize the Americans as much until Banastre Tarleton waged "no-quarter" war in the South two years later.

Wayne escaped injury, but the bloody defeat of his troops so rattled the Continental army that Howe was able to reach Philadelphia unopposed. Moving into the rebel capital, Howe dispatched a large part of his army to the northwest to occupy Germantown in the face of the rebels. Germantown today is just a run-down section of Philadelphia. During the Revolution, it was a section of rolling meadows and grassy estates, inhabited by the well-heeled local gentry.

Throughout their subsequent movements, the American troops remembered what had happened at Paoli. Stories reached them from eyewitnesses of General Grey and his officers tormenting American prisoners, slicing their faces to shreds with their swords before allowing the Light Infantry to bayonet them to death. This same episode would be repeated almost cut for cut a year later when Grey and André cornered Washington's honor guard, Baylor's Dragoons, alongside the Hackensack River in what is now Rivervale, New Jersey. Once again, Grey ordered the flints removed from his men's muskets, and once again the British Light Infantry waded into the American camp with bayonet and musket butt. Once again, eyewitnesses described how the British not only butchered their captives but made sport of them, torturing them with their bayonets before finally killing them.

Actually, Grey and André had no direct involvement in what was to become known as the Baylor Massacre, except that the British Light Infantry under their command once again removed flints from their muskets and surprised Continental soldiers, dispatching them with bayonet and musket butt. The testimony of the survivors of the Baylor Massacre—dragoons under the command of Colonel George Baylor, an intimate of Washington—indicates that the British Light Infantrymen were not content to kill but, rather, tortured and tormented their victims before finally bashing in their heads with musket butts.

The night of September 28, 1778, Colonel Baylor's dragoons moved eastward from Paramus to the west bank of the Hackensack River in what is now Rivervale, New Jersey, in order to scout and observe British troop movements from the enemy's camp at New Bridge (now River Edge). Not finding any British activity, Baylor permitted his dragoons to dismount and bed down in various barns along the river, while he and his adjutant, Major Alexander Clough, commandeered sleeping quarters in a farmhouse. Baylor had unfortunately elected to spend the night in a hotbed of Tory resentment against the rebels, and a local resident took off for New Bridge to inform the British about the presence of the dragoons.

Earlier that same night, the British command had split into two columns for a night march on what they believed was a concentration of rebel forces near Tappan, New York—just a few miles east of where Baylor's men were spending the night. Starting at midnight, Grey and André led a column up the west bank of the Hackensack, along what is now Kinderkamack Road, while another column under Cornwallis moved north between the Hudson and the Hackensack rivers.

Near where Kinderkamack Road crosses Pascack Creek, Grey's column was met by a local Tory who warned the British about the encampment of dragoons a few miles to the east. Grey immediately ordered the Light Infantry to clear the way for an unencumbered march on Tappan. How they did it didn't bother him, but Grey was known to discourage the taking of prisoners.

The Light Infantry slipped quietly behind and around the barns where the dragoons were snoring peacefully, then jumped in with bayonets and musket butts flying. The British worked thoroughly, giving no quarter and taking prisoner only those whom they obviously could not slaughter, such as the wounded Colonel Baylor and Major Clough.

The British wiped off their bayonets and rejoined Grey's force, which moved on to Tappan. Behind them was a scene of bloody carnage that shocked and outraged the Americans. It was reported that more than 50 Americans were butchered, but subsequent research and archeological investigation have revealed that the number of dead was closer to a dozen.

However, the testimony of the survivors, given to Dr. David Griffiths, a Continental army surgeon, indicates clearly that what took place that night was not merely a military action but an atrocity. American dragoons described how they had been prodded and sliced by bayonets despite their pleas of surrender. They reported British officers shouting, "No quarter! No quarter to the damned rebels! No prisoners are to be taken!"

In a report to Major General William Alexander (Lord Stirling), Dr. Griffiths provided a detailed account of what happened, some of which is worth quoting.

The officer who commanded the detachment of the enemy on this service was Major General Grey, who had with him the 2nd light infantry, 2nd grenadiers, the 33rd, and one other regiment of foot and some horse. That he ordered no quarter to be given appears as well as by the enclosed testimony, from the reports of many inhabitants who have heard the British officers speak of it publicly; and also that the charges were drawn from their flintlocks and the flints taken out, that the men might be constrained to the use of their bayonets only. This has occasioned the General to be nick-named, among such of the British officers as can feel the compunctions of humanity, the *No-flint General*. The principal agents of General Grey in this bloody business appear to be a Major

Strawbenzie, Captain Sir James Baird, and a Captain Hall, all of the second light infantry. . . .

It appears that a very few, or none of the British officers entered the quarters of our troops upon this occasion; that no stop might be put to the rage and barbarity of their blood-hounds. It appears, indeed, that *one* of their light infantry had the feelings of remorse and ventured to disobey his order; he gave quarter to the whole fourth troop and not a man of them was hurt, except two that happened to be on guard. For the honor of humanity it is to be wished this gentleman's name had been known.

Notwithstanding the cruelty of the orders, it does not appear that they affected their purpose so fully as they intended or might have been expected. The number of privates present were 104—out of which 11 were killed outright, 17 left behind wounded, 4 of whom are since dead, 39 are prisoners at New York, 8 of them wounded, the rest made their escape.

Of the wounded, Major Clough died, while Baylor lingered on for a few years in bad health before succumbing to his wounds.

Griffiths then submitted to Stirling the following affidavits:

We, the undernamed persons, soldiers in the regiment of light dragoons, commanded by Col. George Baylor, so severally swear and declare solemnly as in the presence of Almighty God that the under-mentioned facts, as related by each of us, are true:

Thomas Hutchinson, Serjeant 3rd troop. He says that he effected his escape unhurt, but as he ran off, he heard the British soldiers cry out '*shiver him*' repeatedly.

Southward Cullency, 1st troop, has twelve wounds, ten of which are in his breast, belly and back. He says that, on the enemy's entering the barn where his troop lay, he and all the men asked for quarter, which was refused; that the British Captain Ball (of the 2nd light infantry) asked his men how many of the rebels were actually dead and, being told the number, he ordered all the rest to be knocked on the head; that the soldiers muttered about it, and asked why they had not been made to kill them all at once, and *why they need have two spells about it?* He adds that five or six of the wounded were knocked on the head.

Thomas Benson, 2nd troop, has twelve wounds, nine of which are in his body, the other three in his arms. He declares that he heard the men in the barn, where he was, ask for quarter, which was returned with wounds and abusive language; that he did not ask for quarter himself, believing it in vain, as he heard the British soldiers reply to the others, who begged it, that their Captain had ordered them to stab all and take no prisoners.

On and on the report goes, detailing the multiple wounds of American dragoons who were stabbed and poked twelve, fifteen times, before being left for dead.*

In the autumn of 1967, a team of professional and amateur archeologists and historians under the direction of Wayne M. Daniels uncovered the skeletons of five of the murdered dragoons; they discovered that at least one of the victims had died from a concussion caused by the bashing in of his skull by a British "Brown Bess" musket.

That André and Grey were responsible for this carnage cannot be proved; however, the fact that it was performed by men under their command is indisputable, just as was the Paoli massacre. The British Light Infantry, with the possible exception of Tory regiments raised by Banastre Tarleton in the South during the later stages of the war, were the toughest, bloodiest fighters in the Revolution. Told to accept no quarter, they did their job efficiently and briskly. From Charles Grey's point of view, the Light

---

* Anyone who doubts the accuracy of this account can verify it in John Almon, *The Remembrancer; or, Impartial Repository of Public Events*, vol. 7 (London, 1779).

Infantry was detached to clear out a possible source of trouble in his march on Tappan, and the Light Infantry carried out his wishes to the fullest. Within less than an hour, Baylor's Dragoons were no longer a threat to Grey, and he and André moved east toward their goal of Tappan.

By the time they arrived, however, the American forces had fled northward and the British were able to occupy the town with no opposition. The prisoners taken during the previous night's raid were lodged in the Tappan Dutch Reformed Church, while one of André's colleagues, Archibald Robertson, climbed a hill to the west of the town and painted a panorama of the Dutch village with the Hudson palisades and highlands in the background. The hill Robertson painted from and the church where the American prisoners were housed would both become part of André's final melodrama two years later.

When the British occupied Philadelphia following the Paoli massacre, André noted with disgust that local farmers would not sell produce to the British because "immediate death is the fate of whomsoever found guilty of bringing any provisions to the British." He proposed adopting the same tactics and hanging any farmer who refused to sell to the British.

"I think were men reduced to the agreeable alternative of choosing by whom they would be hanged, principle alone must turn the scale, so that by threatening at the same rate as the enemy, we should render a whole continent conscientious, a thing devoutly to be wished for."

Grey, accompanied by André and their troops, joined the main British force facing the rebels in Germantown.

While soldiering was a full-time occupation during the

daytime, the British discovered that Philadelphia by night could be most charming. The wealthy families welcomed the British as honored guests, distinct improvements over the less elegant Continental troops who had been in and out of the city while it was the rebel capital. One of the most impressive mansions André visited was Clivedon, the home of Benjamin Chew, a former chief justice of Pennsylvania. The Chews were Tory in their leanings, as many wealthy Philadelphians were, and they welcomed the handsome young captain.

André was immediately attracted to the seventeen-year-old Peggy Chew, with whom he spent much time. He wrote poems to her, but they were not the poetry of a love-sick young man. Rather, they sparkle with the wit of a man who knows exactly where he is going and is not about to get involved romantically until he reaches his goal.

Judging by all contemporary descriptions, André was a very handsome young man. Add to his natural attractiveness the gorgeous red and white uniform of a British staff officer; throw in a sash, sword, spurs, and riding boots; and you have a man who could attract virtually any woman in Philadelphia.

The fact that André knew how attractive he was, added to our own deductions about his ambition, indicates that he was very careful to play with the ladies but not get himself backed into marriage.

Having occupied Philadelphia without firing a shot, the British felt they had won a moral victory that would crush any remaining popular support for the rebel leaders. Capturing Philadelphia was precisely the way William Howe wanted to win the war—by a bloodless show of strength by the awesome British army. If he could show the American people how ridiculous the independence fight was, Howe soon would have the Americans suing for peace.

William Howe was essentially a peaceful man, but even had he thirsted for blood, he would have been distracted by one of the loveliest companions a general could hope for, Mrs. Loring, the wife of Joshua Loring, a British commissary adjutant in Boston. She was delighted by the general's advances, and soon became his mistress. This didn't bother Joshua one whit, for the grateful General Howe promoted him and saw to it that he was well paid.

Howe and his staff were sleeping soundly on the morning of October 4 when, just after daybreak, all of Germantown seemed to explode with the roar of rebel cannon and musketry.

André and Grey, awakened by this sudden firing, rushed out to form their troops into battle line. Dozens of British soldiers came running and limping back through the lines, indicating a powerful American force at their heels. But the Americans missed this one opportunity to rout the British, thanks to a handful of British soldiers who barricaded themselves inside the Chew house, Clivedon, converting it into an impregnable fortress which the Americans could neither capture nor leave uncaptured.

The delay caused by the fighting at the Chew House was all the British needed to organize the troops into fighting units, which methodically swept through Germantown, driving the Americans back and forcing a retreat.

The Battle of Germantown was a loud, smoky, and bloody affair. The Americans lost 53 men trying to storm the Chew House, and the lawn was soaked with blood. Today the Chew House stands quietly, surrounded by a beautiful lawn, a living contrast to the violent struggle for independence.

During this battle, André was in his glory, leading troops against the enemy with bullets whizzing by in the distance. He was in no danger, and he had not yet fought in an engagement where the sides were relatively equal, so it is impossible to call him a battle-seasoned veteran. Actually, this sort of harmless but heroic action was just what André needed to keep his life interesting and exciting.

John André's talents were not those of Benedict Arnold. He conceivably could have become a battlefield commander, but André's expertise was in political maneuvering, behind-the-scenes negotiating, and gathering intelligence about the enemy. One might think that such an ambitious, obviously talented young man would be resented and even disliked, but just the opposite is true. André disguised his ambition, was cordial to all, and soon became known as a powerful intermediary between the troops and General Grey—a function he would later perform to perfection for General Henry Clinton.

Officers and men alike knew that the best route to Grey was through his friendly young aide, and if André promised to look into a matter, the petitioner could expect a reply within a day.

To his fellow officers and superiors, André appeared eager to please. Whenever possible, he would take the initiative and surprise a colleague with a witty little poem in honor of his birthday or the acquisition of a new mistress. If a superior officer received a promotion, André would write and stage a colorful and bawdy little play in honor of the occasion. What we have already seen of the warlike

André was strictly for his *Journal*, wherein he assumed a cold-blooded role in emulation of General Grey, whom he genuinely admired. His letters to his family also reveal this bloody streak, but no one ever saw this while André was living. Even the board of general officers of the American army who tried him regarded André as a polished, civilized young gentleman, a view shared by Washington. The reason for this discrepancy is that André's ferocity was carefully hidden behind the cloak of "No-Flint" Grey. Even when André was egging Grey on to more butchery, it was Grey who collected the infamy, while André curiously escaped blame.

This is the enigma of John André. To all who knew him, he was a warm, witty, charming young man, ambitious but also considerate. There is nothing to indicate the cold viciousness later revealed in his writings. It is possible that he was writing with an eye toward official approval of his professional point of view about soldiering and war. But his captivity in Lancaster and Carlisle certainly provided fuel for a vigorous hatred of the Americans and their ways.

As General Grey's aide he was involved in the Paoli and Baylor massacres, and nowhere in writing does he express the least regret for the violence and bloodshed of these two atrocities. Whether he personally observed them is unprovable historically.

After the battle of Germantown, Captain André settled into Philadelphia society as one of the prominent officers of the British army. André attended parties and moved among the affluent Philadelphians with ease. His easy wit and mastery of the quick impromptu soon made him an invaluable guest at the almost nightly parties. General Grey sent his young aide on his social rounds with a blessing, for the British army could use every friend in America.

Besides, the conquerors of Philadelphia were disturbed by the fireworks and sounds of reveling coming from the nearby American camps. If anything, the rebels should be brooding over their misfortune. Informers told the British staff that the Americans were wildly celebrating a victory by their armies in the north. A victory? It seemed that the rebels were shouting exuberantly and clapping one another on the back over the defeat of the British army at some place called Saratoga. But the British army in the north was invincible under the command of General Burgoyne, and soon would be sweeping southward from Albany to New York along the Hudson River.

Alas, no; Burgoyne had surrendered. Burgoyne *surrendered?* Incredible! A British general might lose a battle, but surrender his entire army to a pack of ill-mannered buffoons with muskets?

Then another piece of information drifted into British headquarters. The American victory had been achieved by the heroic exploits of a former apothecary. This was too much to swallow. Surely the informers must have been paid American agents. No, they were not. The apothecary who had worked a miracle and destroyed the British army in the north was a Connecticut man named Benedict Arnold.

That name sent a chill through André, even while Howe and Grey scoffed at this information. As chief of intelligence, André had heard increasingly disturbing tales about this man Arnold, who seemed to exert a mystical influence over his tatty army as well as the Indians and his

British opponents. André knew that Arnold was the man who had led an army through Maine to storm the impregnable Quebec. This same man, with a skeleton army, had successfully blockaded Quebec until the British garrison was reinforced. Then, by his feats on Lake Champlain, he had stalled the British invasion force long enough to oblige Carleton to return to Quebec and postpone the attack for another year.

While Howe and his generals sniffed contemptuously at the idea of an apothecary holding the mighty British at bay, André was wondering about this strange man whose dedication to the American cause, along with his personal magnetism, had resulted in the surrender of Burgoyne's entire army.

While André was mulling over these questions, his social life remained full. One evening, he attended a party at the home of a prominent Philadelphian who was believed to be a Tory, but who prudently kept his mouth shut about politics, entertaining both Americans and British officers without any obvious show of partiality.

"Captain André, may I present Miss Peggy Shippen. Miss Shippen, Captain André."

7. The Captain, the Tory, and the General

PEGGY SHIPPEN and John André could not have been better suited for one another—not for marriage or a torrid love affair but as close friends and allies. Peggy was nearly eighteen years old, slim, beautiful, and the daughter of a Philadelphia lawyer who in his heart was a Tory but who was determined not to take sides during the Revolution.

André's arrival in Philadelphia on the heels of the harassed American officers—many of whose uniforms were spotted with inelegant patches—was a welcome respite for Peggy. Although her father continually lectured her about getting "involved" (i.e., pregnant) with a British officer, Peggy was delighted to make the acquaintance of such a brilliant, inventive, and clever young man as John André. He escorted her to parties and took her for rides in carriages and sleighs, leaving her at her door at an hour her father thought was disgraceful.

Peggy reassured Edward Shippen again and again that she knew how to take care of herself and was not about to fall prey to those British officers who vowed to sire one bastard for every rebel killed in the war.

Although her family frequently had to leave Philadelphia for temporary exile in New Jersey when patriotic fervor against suspected Tories ran high, Peggy couldn't care less about the financial privations of her father, and she continually demanded that he provide her with expensive dresses, gowns, and coiffures so that she might make a favorable impression on the young bloods of the British army at the nightly parties and balls. When Edward Shippen put down his paternal foot and refused to spend another cent to enhance his daughter's social stature, Peggy had recourse to her favorite ploy—the tantrum.

Peggy's tantrums cowed her father, and later her husband, Benedict Arnold. At eighteen, she was imperious and quick with the coy smile, but equally fast on several occasions to start screaming and heaving crockery when she failed to get her way. Whether these tantrums were fits of temper or manifestations of some deep neurosis is a question best left to psychologists. It is historical fact that she not only was a champion tantrum-thrower but, when necessity pressed, could fake a tantrum that convinced even General Washington and his staff officers.

Peggy's actual relationship with André will probably never be known, because immediately after Benedict's treason was detected, she and her family destroyed all correspondence that might have shed some light on the relationship of the lovely young Philadelphia Tory and the dashing British officer. Novelists can assume historical liberties, but the historian is bound by the lack of evidence to conclude that André and Peggy were only intimate friends. Did Peggy really love André rather than Arnold? It seems unlikely today that such questions can ever be answered with finalty. We can only guess and suppose.

What we do know is that André and Peggy were close and that they continued to correspond after the British left

Philadelphia for New York. We also know that when André returned to New York, he became adjutant general under the new British commander, Sir Henry Clinton, who had replaced General Howe.

Howe's recall to England to explain to Parliament and the War Ministry why he had failed to suppress the American rebellion was a major event during the British occupation of Philadelphia. Since his officers were genuinely fond of him, even when they disagreed with his method of conducting the campaign against Washington's army, "Sir Billy" Howe received one of the most magnificent farewell spectacles any general could wish.

The brilliant young Captain André took charge of arranging the festival, which was called the "Meshianza" (and spelled differently by virtually every participant—including André—and subsequent historians). The motif was medieval knight-errantry, and everyone was costumed along these lines. Only the most beautiful Philadelphia maidens were invited, and naturally Peggy was one of them. André personally supervised the coiffures of the young ladies, many of which were teased to incredible heights.

The girls were to be dressed as Turkish maidens. André specified the details of the costume:

They wore gauze turbans spangled and edged with gold or silver, on the right side a veil of the same kind hung as low as the waist, and the left side of the turban was enriched with pearls and tassels of gold or silver and crested with a feather. The dress was of the Polonaise kind and of white silk with long sleeves. The sashes which were worn around the waist and were tied with a large bow on the left side hung very low and were trimmed, spangled and fringed according to the colors of the knight [whom each accompanied].

Since Peggy was one of three daughters of Edward Shippen who were invited to the ball, he was reluctant to part with so much money for elaborate costuming, especially since he was now living off his savings.

Months were spent preparing a former patriot's mansion to accommodate the cream of the British military aristocracy and the élite of colonial Philadelphia society. There was no need to worry about battling the rebels, who were freezing and starving several miles northwest of Philadelphia on an elevation called Valley Forge. Periodically, rebel units would snipe at the British sentries and outposts, but the cadre of officers organizing the ball in honor of Sir William were oblivious of the actions of the scurvy louts who continued to defy His Majesty.

While preparations for the celebration were nearing completion, the rebels at Valley Forge who had remained faithful to Washington and the American cause suddenly found new hope when they were ordered to form ranks on the parade ground. There they saw a rare sight—the usually grim Washington grinning as his officers read to the men the news that the Battle of Saratoga had indeed won over the French and that King Louis was dispatching troops, munitions, and, most important, gold to help the American cause. From this moment, France was an ally of the Americans and an enemy of Britain.

Sitting alongside Washington and grinning even more broadly was the twenty-year-old French nobleman who was a commissioned major general in the Continental army, Gilbert du Motier, the Marquis de Lafayette. Already regarded by Washington as a son, the red-haired marquis had fought bravely with the Americans and then returned to France to plead with the King to assist his American colleagues. To the persuasions of Benjamin Franklin, who was regarded in France as one of the true *philosophes,* a New World genius, Lafayette added the element of romanticism, which so appealed to a French court sunk in the depths of cynicism. With alacrity, many of the Marquis's fellow noblemen—most of whom would die on the guillotine during the French Revolution fifteen years later —hurried to lend their talents and wealth to the American cause.

But aside from an occasional cannon blast or skyrocket display, little that came from the American encampment dimmed the enthusiasm of Captain André as he feverishly completed the final preparations for General Howe's farewell.

One snag threatened to spoil the affair, but André was not about to let anything ruin what he had so elaborately confected. Edward Shippen had been thinking hard about the money he would have to put out for his daughters' costumes, and a visit by some local Quakers who deplored the licentiousness of the British scheme seemed to convince him. He summoned his daughters on the eve of the ball and told them that they would not attend. They pleaded, then yelled, then screamed, and finally broke down into tears of rage. Several hours later, a British officer arrived at the house to pick up the costumes they had so lovingly worked on, in order to give them to other women to fill in for the three Shippen daughters.

Peggy's tantrum was probably the highlight of that evening in the Shippen house, but for once Edward refused to give in to his spoiled favorite and her sisters. In a different colonial setting, the father might have strapped such impudent daughters to the point of tears, but Edward

Shippen was not a violent man, and he quietly endured their protestations. But the girls stayed home while the British celebrated.

The Meshianza was, by all contemporary accounts, a spectacular success. André and his fellow officers spared no expense to provide General Howe and his friends an evening they would never forget. Pageantry was followed by a fireworks display unseen before in America.

The rebels came close to spoiling the party when a small detachment of Washington's forces slipped among the British ammunition supplies at Germantown and blew them up with an explosion that rocked the hall where the revelers were. Several British officers, realizing what had happened, slipped quietly away from the party and attempted to pursue the Americans, but they were laughed at in their ridiculous costumes, and rebel musketry got too hot for the British. Meanwhile, Howe and André had been reassuring the guests that the explosions were part of the festive fireworks and had been designed to scare the rebels.

Shortly after Howe's departure for England, his successor, Sir Henry Clinton, ordered the British troops to evacuate Philadelphia and return to New York. This departure spelled the end of an important phase of John André's career. While in Philadelphia, he wrote plays and poetry, flirted with the eligible women, and won the friendship of Peggy Shippen, with whom he promised to correspond regularly from New York. His future was uncertain, for Grey, weary of the no-win policy of British generals in America, announced to his young aide that he had decided to return to England. However, he did promise to recommend him to Sir Henry. Grey's warm endorsement of André's talents convinced Clinton, and he appointed the brilliant captain first as his aide, then the adjutant general, thus making him the second most important man in the British army, even though he was outranked by many other officers.

For Peggy, the departure of the British meant a farewell to the opulent balls and festivals. She and her family knew that the British would be followed by the Americans, and there was not an American officer as witty or charming or talented as John André. Before he left, he had her pose for one of his famous pen-and-ink sketches. With her hair teased almost twice the size of her head, Peggy stares out at posterity with the hint of a smile, a self-assured young lady who obviously knew precisely what was best for Peggy Shippen and was determined to get it.

During the months that André had been entrancing Peggy, the wounded Benedict Arnold was recuperating at Saratoga. Moments before he passed out from the pain in his leg following his storming of the Breymann redoubt, Arnold had sternly ordered the battle surgeons not to amputate his leg, as they desired. His convalescence was stormy, filled with indignant letters to friends and fellow officers protesting Gates's treatment of him, alternating with angry outbursts to any visitor. When, on November 29, 1777, Congress finally authorized Washington to restore Arnold's rank and seniority, it was a case of too little too late. It took Washington several weeks to sort through his official papers and finally notify Arnold officially of his restoration, and this delay further annoyed the belligerent general. Why should Washington take so long to communicate to him what friends had reported weeks earlier?

During his stay in the hospital, with his wounded leg strapped to a board and being unable to move about freely,

Arnold divided his waking hours among writing indignant letters, harranguing his visitors, and stewing over the injustices heaped upon him. No matter what he did, someone seemed determined to criticize his conduct or, worse, ignore his achievements. And, unfortunately for Arnold, the staff surrounding him was composed of men who had no love for "Granny" Gates—as his enemies called him—and they continually fed his bitterness.

There was nothing unique about Arnold the man. Anyone of a mercurial, flamboyant, dashing disposition, when deprived of recognition, becomes paranoid very easily. This happens every day to men in education, politics, military service, government jobs, actors, playwrights, authors, and many, many others. Those whose genius is self-contained and not dependent on others still need applause and encouragement. When overlooked or ignored, they stew in agony.

By the time Benedict Arnold was well enough to travel by carriage to join Washington's army the following spring, he was a profoundly bitter man, convinced of his own self-righteousness and with a large chip on his shoulder.

André was making last-minute preparations for the Meshianza, and Peggy and her sisters were still being fitted for their costumes, when Arnold's coach pulled up in front of Washington's headquarters at Valley Forge. Four men had to help the wounded veteran out of the coach, but he waved them aside as he took his crutches and advanced toward where Washington was staying. Alerted by his aides that Arnold had arrived, Washington waived his customary formality and ran down the steps to embrace Arnold in a bear hug.

Then, after seeing that Arnold was comfortable,

Washington complimented him on the restoration of his rank and seniority and praised him for his valor at Saratoga. Realizing that his best field general would be incapable of military action for several months, Washington appointed Arnold military commander of Philadelphia once the British left, which American intelligence reports indicated would be any day now. Arnold smiled in gratitude for this gesture on Washington's part, although the commander in chief could not have made a worse selection.✗

Arnold was a battlefield hero, but as an administrator he was hopelessly incompetent, reacting harshly one moment, then behaving with extreme humanity the next. He could never keep his personal finances separate from the army funds which he had to oversee—a flaw Washington should have known clearly from all the uproar over Arnold's expense accounting during the Ticonderoga and Quebec expeditions. But Washington wanted to honor his brave friend and gave him the wrong job, thus unwittingly setting the stage for the Arnold-Peggy-André conspiracy.

To unravel Arnold's financial disasters at this point in history requires the analyses of accountants. He invested in a privateer, then requisitioned army wagons to carry the goods from the privateer to Philadelphia, where he sold them at a handsome profit. There was nothing illegal or immoral in privateer speculation (Washington himself entered into such arrangements), and Arnold intended to pay for the use of the army wagons from his own pocket.

Arnold corresponded secretly with New York merchants about various business deals, and it became difficult to sort out his personal affairs from his military duties. His first mistake was to move into the sumptuous mansion recently occupied by General Howe, complete with a full staff of servants, cooks, and maids. He dashed around Philadelphia in an extravagant coach, determined to impress upon the haughtier Philadelphians that a former apothecary from Connecticut was now lord and master of their destinies. He ordered all stores shut until his men had had a chance to "requisition" (i.e., steal) from them any necessary goods. This did little to endear Arnold to the city he was governing.

Like the British officers, Arnold was determined to enjoy Philadelphia society to the hilt, and he took particular pleasure in the attention he received every time he would enter a party, hobble to a conveniently placed chair, rest his wounded leg on a cushion, and regale the younger officers and the melting maidens with his exploits at Quebec and Saratoga. Arnold at last was in his element, even though by day he was hopelessly bungling the military management of the city as well as his own affairs. To hell with those disgruntled civilians, especially Joseph Reed, president of the Supreme Executive Council of Pennsylvania, who seemed to file a complaint against Arnold daily with Washington or with Congress.

Arnold sat back comfortably, nursing a token drink while watching his officers dance. That he was unable to sweep around the dance floor bothered him not one whit, for while others danced, there was invariably a small crowd of young ladies who doted on the darkly handsome hero. One of these caught his eye quickly and held it, never letting go. At party after party, Arnold found himself in a deep, unspoken communication with Peggy Shippen, whose eyes seemed to answer all the questions he had been asking himself for years about the ideal woman.

Forsaking his daytime duties, General Arnold managed

to pay several visits to the Shippen house, chatting politely with the slightly boring Edward Shippen but continually exchanging glances with Peggy. He took her for rides through the city and the countryside around Philadelphia, and soon all the city knew that the hero of Saratoga, the Dark Eagle, was in love.

The courtship was spirited, with Arnold impetuously proposing and Peggy coyly declining. Refusing to be daunted now that he had found the perfect mate, Arnold renewed his pursuit. To Peggy, this was a match that she had not imagined, hoping instead to ultimately marry a wealthy British officer with a promising career. But here was the hero of heroes of an army whose cause she secretly despised, yet whose magnetism was so powerful that she could not turn away from him.

Edward Shippen tried to discourage Peggy, pointing out that Arnold was nearly twenty years her senior and that his future was by no means secure. True, he had risen above his middle-class origins and showed a definite ability to make money, but his financial management and the seeming conflict of interests which were discussed in select Philadelphia circles made him seem a shaky prospect as a son-in-law, especially as a husband for the spoiled Peggy.

For the thirty-seven-year-old, raven-haired major general, Peggy's coyness was typical of the young women of Philadelphia. Benjamin Franklin's daughter, Sarah Franklin Bache, wrote to her father in Paris that Arnold was impressed with the kissing ability of her one-year-old daughter, Betty.

"You can't think how fond of kissing she is, and gives such old-fashioned smacks. General Arnold says he would give a good deal to have her for a schoolmistress to teach the ladies how to kiss."

Robert Morris's wife wrote of the Arnold-Peggy courtship that "Cupid has given our little general a more mortal wound than all the host of Britons could."

At five feet seven inches, Arnold could hardly be described during the colonial era as "little," except when compared with such relative giants as George Washington and Ethan Allen, both of whom were over six feet tall.

Social Philadelphia learned about Arnold's impassioned courtship of the eighteen-year-old Tory beauty, and gossip buzzed about the possible outcome. Arnold gloried in his position of military governor of Philadelphia and spent money freely. His credit was good, and he abused it to the utmost. There were murmurings in Philadelphia of accusations against him concerning conflicts of interest and profiteering. Also, there was that old feud with Congress over his rank and seniority. The Dark Eagle was indeed a hero, but a somewhat tarnished idol because of the number of whispers and accusations circulating in military and social circles. Rumors are always difficult to document, since no one wants to claim credit for originating what might prove slanderous.

True to his nature, Arnold contemptuously dismissed all the nasty rumors as the work of his enemies, and he continued his pursuit of the lovely Peggy Shippen. It would be like Arnold to hobble brusquely from his office and tell his secretary to cancel the rest of his appointments while he paid court to Peggy. Those who had been waiting for an audience with the military governor naturally felt slighted and added fuel to the fire being built under Arnold.

But Arnold seemed to keep the wolves at bay while he continued his determined courtship. Finally yielding to the siege of the hero of Saratoga, Peggy consented to become Arnold's second wife. Edward Shippen had already given his approval.

As a gesture to Peggy of how he planned to treat her —and also as an indication that he had given up his hopes of securing a large grant of former Tory property in northern New York—Arnold on March 22, 1779, purchased Mount Pleasant, a lovely mansion overlooking the river and part of what is now Fairmount Park in Philadelphia. Although Arnold and Peggy never lived there, he planned to move in eventually and settled the estate on himself and Peggy for their lives.

On April 8, Peggy became Arnold's bride in a simple ceremony in the Shippen house, with the still wounded general having to be supported by a soldier during the ceremony, and during the reception he sat with his leg propped up on a campstool.

8. *Arnold Under Attack*

ARNOLD'S ENEMIES were gathering like a wolf pack. They were led by Joseph Reed, president of the Pennsylvania council, and Joseph Matlack, secretary of the council. Arnold had run afoul of Matlack in October, 1778, when Arnold's aide, Major David Franks, ordered Matlack's son William, a sergeant in the militia, to go fetch a barber for him. Young Matlack thought that was too demeaning a task for one of his rank, so he complained to his influential father, who promptly wrote to Arnold. In reply, Arnold stressed the limitations of individual freedom among soldiers during warfare.

No man has a higher sense of the rights of a citizen and freeman than myself. They are dear to me, as I have fought and bled for them, and as it is my highest ambition and most ardent wish to resume the character of a free citizen whenever the service of my country will permit.

At the same time, let me observe, that whenever necessity obliges the citizen to assume the character of a soldier, the former is entirely lost in the latter, and the respect due to the citizen is by no means to be paid to the soldier any further than his rank entitles him to it; this is evident from the necessity of military discipline, the basis of which is implicit obedience, and however the feelings of a citizen may be hurt, he has this consolation, that it is a sacrifice he pays to the safety of his country.

This letter enraged the elder Matlack, who threatened to pull his son out of the militia and publish the reasons for his action. Arnold calmly replied that if such remarks were intended as a threat, "you have mistaken your object. I am not to be intimidated by a newspaper. To vindicate the rights of citizens I became a soldier and bear the marks upon me; I hope your candor will acquit me of the inconsistence of invading what I have fought and bled to defend."

Arnold's letter was a minature masterpiece, for it not only told Matlack to keep his civilian nose out of military matters but also informed him whom he had been addressing. Many other men would have hesitated before taking on the formidable Benedict Arnold—a man whose patriotism and heroism could be denied by none—but Matlack was not one of them. He and his fellow councilmen drew up a list of charges against Arnold and sent copies not only to Congress and to General Washington but to the leaders of all the other states and every newspaper.

Arnold had been on his way north to Poughkeepsie to negotiate with New York politicians the large land grant he was hoping for when news of the Pennsylvania council's action reached him. He immediately detoured to Middlebrook, New Jersey, Washington's current headquarters after he broke winter quarters at Valley Forge. Washington greeted his impetuous friend warmly and, after listening to Arnold's account of his persecution, urged Arnold to demand a court martial to clear the air of these charges once and for all.

The two charges that were to haunt Arnold concerned the *Charming Nancy*, a schooner, and his use of army wagons to carry the ship's cargo to Philadelphia. At this distance in time, the whole affair seems rather petty, but at the same time it fanned the flames of anti-Arnold feeling, especially among the members of the Pennsylvania council and in particular Joseph Reed, who felt that he alone had the right to issue passes.

Briefly, what happened was that the schooner, owned by Americans, wanted to land its goods in Philadelphia, and one of its owners, Robert Shewall, visited Arnold at Valley Forge—after he had been named military commander of the city—and requested a pass, which Arnold granted.

Meanwhile, the *Charming Nancy* was captured by an American pirate and sailed into Egg Harbor, New Jersey. Then the British made a sudden attack on the port and Arnold—apparently as part of a deal made earlier with Shewall—requisitioned twelve government wagons to bring as much as possible of her cargo back to Philadelphia for sale, the profits to be split fifty-fifty between Shewall and Arnold.

Arnold maintained that he fully intended to pay for the use of the wagons to haul what was considered private property, and the Philadelphia quartermaster said that the army suffered no inconvenience by Arnold's use of the wagons at that time. It seems clear that while Arnold might not have exercised the best judgment, considering his important position, he certainly was not criminal in his actions.

There were eight charges brought against Arnold by the Pennsylvania council. The first concerned his issuing a pass to the schooner without first consulting Joseph Reed or the council. The second was that he had closed all stores in Philadelphia—which he had done with Washington's permission in order for the army to buy enough equipment and stores—but that he himself had "privately made considerable purchases for his own benefit."

The third charge concerned his treatment of young Matlack. The fourth charge involved some hazy dealings having to do with the sloop *Active*, a charge so vague that it was the first to be thrown out by Congress. The fifth accusation was about his use of the army wagons. The sixth was that he had usurped the civilian powers of the Pennsylvania council by writing a pass for someone to cross into enemy lines. The seventh accused him of making "an indecent and disrespectful refusal" to explain his use of the wagons to the council, and the eighth charge was a general attack on his character, claiming that he favored loyalists.

In presenting the charges against Arnold, the Pennsylvania council rashly threatened not to release troops or supplies to Arnold upon his return as military commandant of Philadelphia.

It is interesting to note from our historical vantage point that the man most vilified today by conservative, patriotic organizations was, during his tenure in Philadelphia, strongly identified with the landed gentry of the political right. The Pennsylvania radicals and democratic levelers warmly disliked Arnold, who sneered publicly at the concept of an army run on democratic principles. He was fighting for freedom—the freedom of the individual from unwarranted oppression and interference by the state. Arnold was a businessman, one of America's earliest capitalists, and any notion that would deny him the fruits of his investments and machinations received his scorn.

Arnold the general and soldier fought fiercely for independence, but Arnold the businessman was not fighting for a democratic concept in social or economic terms. It comes as no surprise that Arnold's first literary champion, novelist Kenneth Roberts, himself believed strongly in the freedom of the individual from governmental restraints.

Matlack and his colleagues on the Pennsylvania council were so determined to vilify Arnold that they resurrected Major Brown's old broadside alleging that Arnold had looted the citizens of Montreal and cheated his own troops to enhance his personal fortune. The council instructed the Pennsylvania delegation to Congress to demand the immediate ouster of Arnold as military commander, but none of the delegates from the other states agreed. Instead, the motion was referred to a committee, which leisurely studied it and the supposed evidence and then, on March 17, reported that only four of the charges against Arnold could be tried by a court-martial, and that of these four only two could possibly be proven. That same day Arnold petitioned Congress for an immediate court-martial, and two days later he tendered his resignation as military commander of Philadelphia. Congress instructed Washington to call together a board of officers to try the charges against the general.

On April 20, 1779, Washington set May 1 as the date for the court-martial. The Pennsylvania council protested that Washington was not giving them enough time to assemble every piece of evidence against Arnold. So the date was pushed back, first to June 1, then to July 1.

These delays infuriated the sensitive Arnold, who felt

that Congress was pressuring Washington to give every possible advantage to the Pennsylvanians. Finally, on May 5, Arnold wrote hysterically to Washington:

If Your Excellency thinks me criminal, for heaven's sake let me be immediately tried and, if found guilty, executed. I want no favour; I ask only justice. . . . I have nothing left but the little reputation I have gained in the army. Delay in the present case is worse than death. . . . I entreat that the court may be ordered to sit as soon as possible.

When both sides were finally ready, summer had arrived and the British were coming out of their hibernation and once again waging war against the rebels. The court-martial did not convene until after the summer campaign, when Washington and his army were safely snuggled in winter quarters in the New Jersey hills around Morristown. On December 25, 1779, the hearings opened, and continued sporadically until the following January 26.

Arnold chose to defend himself—with frequent allusions to the wounds he had suffered in his country's service—against all the charges against him, including those that Congress had dismissed as being not worthy of investigation. But to criticize Benedict Arnold was to draw from him the fullest possible defense.

He defended his issuance of a safe-conduct pass to the *Charming Nancy*, the ship which he had permitted to land its goods in American-held territory (omitting the fact that he subsequently acquired a handsome share in the ship's ownership).

Against the charge that he had looted the Philadelphia stores and shops during the two days after his arrival when he had closed them down in order to procure from them goods necessary for the army, Arnold merely said that he was acting under congressional authority. Once again, he neglected to tell the court-martial about a secret bargain he had made with merchants James Mease and William West to share with them in the sale of confiscated goods the army could not use.

The most serious charge—that of appropriating military wagons to haul his private goods—Arnold answered by claiming that he had intended from the start to pay for their use from his own pocket.

On January 26, the court cleared Arnold of all charges except the pass to the *Charming Nancy* and the use of the public wagons. In its verdict, the court noted:

. . . it also appears that General Arnold intended this application as a private request and that he had no design of employing the wagons otherwise than at his private expense, nor of defrauding the public, nor injuring or impeding the public service, but considering the delicacy attending the high station in which the general acted, and that requests from him might operate as commands, they [the board] are of the opinion the request was imprudent and improper and that, therefore, it ought not to have been made. The court . . . do sentence him to receive a reprimand from his Excellency the commander-in-chief.

On February 12, 1780, Congress approved the court's verdict but did not communicate this approval to Washington for several weeks. On April 6, Washington acceded to Congress and sent Arnold a formal letter.

The Commander-in-chief would have been much happier in an occasion of bestowing commendations on an officer who has rendered such distinguished services to his country as Major General Arnold; but in the present case a sense of duty and a regard to candor oblige him to declare that he considers his conduct in the instance of the permit [to the *Charming Nancy*], as peculiarly reprehensible, both in a civil and military view, and in the affair of the wagons as "imprudent and improper."

How that letter must have disturbed Washington! The court and Congress had both passed on to him the obligation to censure his bravest, most imaginative general. It is not necessary to read between the lines to see Washington easing the blow to Arnold's vanity. Even when it came to the matter of the wagons, Washington merely parroted the phrase of the court, refusing to elaborate on what he probably regarded as a minor incident which had been blown up so far out of proportion as to seriously cripple the morale of the already physically crippled Arnold.

From the point of view of Arnold's bride, Peggy, and his friends, this reprimand was the ultimate disgrace to a brave man. From the vantage point of nearly two hundred years, we can see that Arnold was an incorrigible schemer and had entered several business deals which might have caused the board of officers trying him to be more severe in their censure. However, nothing that Arnold had done so far could have justified anything more than a strongly worded reprimand from Washington.

Nothing, that is, except a conversation he had with the proprietor of a Philadelphia glass-and-china shop in May of 1779—only weeks after his marriage to Peggy Shippen and possibly just days before or after his hysterical letter of May 5 to Washington begging to be executed if found guilty. Had that conversation between Arnold and Joseph Stansbury been reported during his trial, Washington would have been more than willing to grant Arnold's request.

9. *Arnold Turns*

"BETWEEN HIS VICTORY AT Saratoga in the fall of 1777 and his letter to Washington in May of 1779, Benedict Arnold's world was dark." The excruciating pain of the wound in his left leg, which was mending very slowly (and probably very poorly, considering the seriousness of his wound and the primitive techniques available), was briefly assuaged by Washington's warm recognition of Arnold's achievements and Arnold's Philadelphia appointment. But even when success surrounded him, Arnold was deep in debt and involved in numerous dealings that were shady at best but which he considered necessary to maintain an income to suport him in the luxury he felt he deserved. Also, he had his three boys to educate and support.

His courtship of Peggy was certainly a bright moment, but even that was overcast by the growls of the Pennsylvania council and the increasing accusations against him.

The exact moment when Benedict Arnold finally broke under the pressure will probably never be known, for he and Peggy and Peggy's family destroyed every scrap of potentially incriminating evidence when Arnold went over to the British. It wasn't until 1941, with the publication of Carl Van Doren's *Secret History of the American Revolu-*

tion—an analysis of the British Army Headquarters Papers —that it was revealed to the world that while Arnold was writing frantically to Washington and to his friends protesting his loyalty, he had already taken the first step toward joining the British, and Van Doren's study clearly demonstrates the strong role Peggy played in Arnold's decision.

The closest time we can approximate for Arnold's loss of faith in the American cause was when his court-martial was announced for May 1, then twice delayed. Had Congress thrown out the accusations against Arnold in the first place as being unworthy of investigation and court-martial, Arnold would probably have remained a loyal American general and . . . but it is fruitless to speculate about where Benedict Arnold might have stood today in our national hagiology.

The postponement of the court-martial from May to June probably confirmed in Arnold's mind what had already taken root there when Congress approved the trial. This action, following months of harassment by the Pennsylvanians, and the resuscitation of Brown's old charges, were enough to tip the hypersensitive Arnold in the direction in which his young Tory bride was luring him.

At this point in the account of Benedict Arnold's career, American historians tend to assume that Arnold was possessed by some devil or that his nascent cupidity siezed control of the hero of Quebec, Valcour Island, and Saratoga. It seems difficult for a patriotic American to imagine that Benedict Arnold might have been justified —if only to himself—in changing sides.

From the British point of view, Arnold was a renegade who was merely returning to his true allegiance to King George. "Treason" and "loyalty." "Traitor" and "patriot." These can only be words to the historian. Was Benedict Arnold more reprehensible than the many Americans who remained loyal to the Crown and joined Tory regiments just because he changed sides once the war was on?

These are not idle questions but vital ones that must at least be acknowledged by anyone who pretends to write an honest, impartial account of Benedict Arnold. It is not the purpose of this book to glorify or vilify Arnold, but rather to try to peer inside the man's tormented soul to understand why he did what he did.

Henry Steele Commager and Richard B. Morris, in their otherwise excellent two-volume *The Spirit of 'Seventy-Six*, follow the familiar pattern of praising Arnold's military achievements but . . .

Why, then, did he go over to the enemy? His own explanation—that he was outraged by the French alliance and in despair over the American cause—cannot be accepted; it came too late. Aside from this rationalization there were two motives or pressures to which Arnold responded: resentment against real and imagined slights by the Congress and by the authorities of Pennsylvania; reckless extravagance and a desperate need for money. A court-martial had just reprimanded him for improper conduct bordering on corruption. Yet all American generals who felt slighted and who needed money did not turn traitor; in fact none did but Arnold. Clearly the ultimate explanation is to be found in the mysterious realm of personality. Arnold was a man without principles or convictions, a gambler, hot-headed, reckless, arrogant and ambitious.

We know that treason is heinous and should be punished, and that such treason as Arnold's should bring odium and remorse. There is no evidence that it did.

This is the sort of pious patriotic sentiment which permeates everything written about Benedict Arnold. The American historian just has to get in those canards about Arnold's lack of principles and the heinousness of treason.

And as they fill with moral indignation, historians lose the objectivity and detachment so essential for an honest study of a controversial man. There can be no question that Benedict Arnold was more than willing to make a profit on whatever deals he concocted during the Revolution, yet it is also true that he spent his own money freely during the march on Quebec and the Lake Champlain campaign. Perhaps he did pad his expenses a bit, but in this he was magnificently exceeded by His Excellency General Washington, who refused a salary on condition that Congress pay his expenses—an arrangement that brought the General considerably more money than any salary. (Marvin Kitman has delightfully—and accurately—analyzed Washington's padding in his *George Washington's Expense Account*.)

In fairness to Benedict Arnold, let us assume that for many complicated reasons he decided to change sides in a war and had the misfortune to pick the losing side.

The unquestionable fact is that in May of 1779, while he was awaiting a court-martial, Arnold entered into negotiations to join the British army. In some of his early letters he signed himself "Monk," after the British General George Monk of Cromwell's army who, following the death of Cromwell, secretly negotiated with the royalists to lead the way to the restoration of the monarchy under King Charles II. Monk won for himself the esteem of his countrymen and a dukedom from his grateful sovereign.

With such a historical example of a victorious renegade before him, Arnold could not help but think that the cause he had been fighting for—as Monk had valiantly fought with Cromwell against the monarchy—had now been exhausted and the time was ripe to reconcile battling countrymen with one swift stroke by a military genius.

Monk's heroic deed had taken place little more than a century before, and its significance was still fresh in the mind of Benedict Arnold. Monk had recognized the collapse of the republican government he had helped Oliver Cromwell to erect, following the execution of Charles I in 1649. The decapitation of the King of England, God's anointed regent on earth, spelled out forcibly to all Englishmen that the divine rights of kings was dead and that rule by the people had arrived. Unfortunately for England, Oliver Cromwell betrayed the republican principles he had espoused in order to get rid of the monarchy and installed himself as Lord Protector of England—that is, dictator. With Cromwell's sovereignty came the rule of the Puritans, which meant shutting down the theaters, blue laws prohibiting commerce on the Sabbath (Sunday by Christian reckoning), and a reign of religious oppression. By the time of Cromwell's death, the English people were heartily fed up with the Puritans, and General Monk's magnificent defection was applauded by a grateful Parliament.

In Benedict Arnold's case, however, the American people were not that fed up with the efforts of the Continental Congress to establish an independent government to rule the thirteen American states. Had Arnold decided to defect in 1776, or had the Americans defied international feelings by executing a divine monarch, the sway of public opinion might have gone with Arnold. But the Americans had merely cut themselves free from King George by a written document and by arming themselves against the British army, and in no way did they endanger the health or life of His Majesty.

Historians have puzzled over Arnold's selection of Joseph Stansbury as the man to convey his first overtures to Sir Henry Clinton. Stansbury was known as a loyalist during the British occupation of Philadelphia, yet when the Americans took control of the city, he willingly signed the oath of allegiance to the United States. It is possible that André, before he left, had told Peggy that Stansbury was a man to be trusted.

Early in May of 1779, Arnold sent for the glass-and-china merchant, and "after some general conversation," Stansbury wrote after the war, Arnold "opened his political sentiments respecting the war carrying on between Great Britain and America, declaring his abhorrence of a separation of the latter from the former as a measure that would be ruinous to both."

Stansbury continued that Arnold "then communicated to me, under a solemn obligation of secrecy, his intention of opening his services to the commander-in-chief of the British army or co-operating on some concealed plan with Sir Henry Clinton."

Arnold made it clear to Stansbury that he would work with Clinton in any capacity to overturn Congress and restore British rule in America.

Stansbury left for New York, where he recruited the help of a fellow Tory, Jonathan Odell, a clergyman and physician with good connections in the British general headquarters.

On the morning of May 10, Odell arranged a meeting between Stansbury and General Clinton's young aide, Captain John André. Arnold had impressed on Stansbury the importance of the British fighting the war through to a successful conclusion. Otherwise his offer would not stand.

André, who prided himself on his intelligence reports about disaffection among the American troops and their officers, was stunned by this offer of the enemy's greatest general to join the British army. André assured Stansbury that the British had no intention of abandoning the war, and then worked out general terms of an agreement whereby the British would welcome Arnold and, should he deliver into their hands a large number of rebel troops, Arnold could expect His Majesty's gratitude to be measurable. André told Stansbury, who had to return immediately to Philadelphia, that he would give the matter his immediate attention and draw up a letter setting forth the points of their agreement.

It is interesting to note that André committed the British to accepting Arnold's offer without even checking first with Sir Henry. This was not brashness or presumption on the young aide's part, but rather a measure of their mutual trust. Clinton had come to depend on André so strongly that he would shortly appoint him to the post of adjutant general of the British army. André was able to think as Clinton thought, and he instinctively knew he had made the right decision. Before writing Stansbury that same day, André discussed the matter with Clinton, who apparently gave his aide permission to continue.

Writing to Stansbury that same day, André was concise.

On our part we meet Monk's overtures with full reliance on his honourable intentions and disclose to him with the strongest assurances of our sincerity that no thought is entertained of abandoning the point we have in view. That on the contrary, powerful means are expected for accomplishing our end.

André goes on the assure "Monk" that his defection and deliverance of "an obnoxious band of men" would be suitably rewarded. Nothing is said about money or titles, but André makes several references to gratitude, honor, and rewards. Then, in a chillingly prophetic sentence, André adds that should Arnold's "manifest efforts be foiled and after every zealous attempt flight be at length necessary, the cause in which he suffers will hold itself bound to indemnify him for his losses and receive him with the honour his conduct deserves.

"His own judgement will point out the services required, but for his satisfaction we give the following hints."

André spelled out how he and Arnold would communicate through Stansbury. They would write in cipher, using Blackstone's *Commentaries* as the code book. Each word in the letter would be indicated by three numbers which would indicate the page, the number of the line on the page, and the number of the word in that line.

There was nothing André enjoyed more than high-level conspiracy, and he played the master spy to the hilt. In addition to writing in cipher, the two could also write seemingly innocent letters, but with important messages tucked between the lines in invisible ink, which could be developed by using either acid or heat from a flame. Therefore, each such letter would be marked with an

"A" for acid or an "F" for fire.

Also, André immediately opened a correspondence with Peggy. André would write chatty little notes about women's fashions in New York, and Peggy Arnold would reply with local gossip and references to the Meshianza, with each note interlined in invisible ink.

In his draft of the letter to Stansbury, André had started to write "Arnold," but crossed it out and replaced it with "Monk." Stansbury got the copy, while the original remained in the headquarters files. André saw to it that Clinton received a copy of the letter for his approval.

That draft, incidentally, is the first recorded document of the great conspiracy. It is dated May 10, 1779, clearly revealing that while Arnold was bitterly defending his integrity and honor to General Washington he had already taken the first steps toward transferring his allegiance. Although Arnold had offered, via Stansbury, to defect immediately, he also suggested the alternative of staying in the American service long enough to make his switch of sides at a time when it could do the greatest harm to the American cause and offer the greatest benefit to the British. This latter course apparently appealed to Sir Henry, for at no point in the early correspondence does André suggest an immediate defection.

During the 160 years that the Clinton Papers remained hidden from the public, many theories were advanced for Arnold's decision to change sides. One romantic theory held that André had been a lover of Peggy Shippen's and had carefully set up the whole business and manipulated Arnold as a puppet. But the evidence is overwhelming that Arnold initiated the move and that André and Clinton were surprised. That Peggy played a major role in the decision is not to be doubted, but whether she first planted the thought in Arnold's mind or merely encouraged his own decision will probably never be known.

Arnold knew from the start he was playing a deadly game. His lameness was a real enough excuse to keep him out of battle during the summer campaign of 1779, and it gave him time to correspond in detail with the British and iron out such important matters as his compensation, his rank in the British army, and the timetable for his defection.

Both sides took elaborate precautions in their correspondence, with André signing his letters "John Anderson" and Arnold adopting various pseudonyms such as "Moore" and "Gustavus." The fact that the negotiations continued for almost a year and a half indicates Arnold's conviction that the British would ultimately win. Had the Americans shown a sudden surge of strength, it would have been simple for him to abandon the plot. And if it was later detected, he could claim that he had undertaken an espionage mission in order to befuddle the British high command and deliberately feed them misleading information—a course of action that Washington frequently followed by sending phony defectors into the British lines.

.   It is probable that Arnold convinced himself of the rightness of his move as the war dragged out without any resolution in sight. As for the possibility of his being called a traitor, Arnold could console himself with the oft-quoted observation of Sir John Harrington, "If it prosper, none dare call it treason."

10. Hard Bargaining

IN RECOUNTING the events and accidents which ultimately brought together two such brilliant men as Benedict Arnold and John André, chronological sequence sometimes suffers. In the last chapter we saw André functioning as Sir Henry Clinton's right-hand man, negotiating directly with Arnold. However, the last previous mention of him was in his role as organizer of the gala farewell to General Howe and as General Grey's aide-de-camp.

Grey had taken a long look at Clinton and decided that he was as ineffective as Howe in prosecuting the war, and Grey decided to return to England at the next possible opportunity. However, he had become sufficiently fond of his young aide to want to further his career by calling him to Clinton's attention.

Sir Henry Clinton was decidedly not a gregarious man. Shy, aloof, and often indecisive, he refused to let anyone get really close to him. His only moments of abandon were during those boisterous winter months in a tattered and fire-ravaged Manhattan when he and some of his officers would drink themselves into a stupor while frolicking with prostitutes. He and his staff were known to be virtually unapproachable until the previous night's hangovers dissipated, but Clinton, who had appointed André as one of his staff aides, was pleasantly surprised to find André ready to work first thing in the morning and throughout the day with an indefatigable energy and charm. It was André's charm that ultimately won him Clinton's admiration, confidence, and friendship. André did not insinuate himself as a sycophant or boot-kicker, but rather caught the eye of the commander in chief by his efficiency and his willingness to take on the burdensome paper work that Clinton despised.

Also, André maneuvered himself into a position of control of British intelligence, sifting out the useless information brought by would-be spies and presenting to Clinton only what he knew to be reliable intelligence reports.

During the evenings, André often spent his hours at the theater, staging comedies, writing witty verse, and even acting. He definitely was a young officer on his way up, and older officers on Clinton's staff did not take kindly to this climber. Yet his efficiency and willingness to work tirelessly while the rest of them went out and got drunk did not escape Clinton's notice, and little by little Captain André worked himself to the point where, when the adjutant general resigned, he was the best-qualified man for the post. Clinton appointed him, and André purchased a commission as major.

During the winter of 1778–79, when Arnold's resentment was building to fever pitch almost in direct proportion to the heat of his courtship of Peggy, a disgusted General Charles Grey returned to England in the hope of obtaining a command where he could wage war as a civilized soldier should—with fire and sword. But before he left, Grey had the pleasure of seeing his young friend on the staff of General Clinton.

Clinton's other staff aides were generally so corrupt as to make André stand out as a model of efficiency and integrity. Since he was financially comfortable, André had no truck with the incessant bribery, graft, and financial scheming that made Clinton's administration reek of corruption. And since Clinton, like Howe before him, had an aversion to Grey's type of bloody warfare, André appealed to his sympathies with strong-worded orders for Clinton's signature condemning the practice of looting and plundering. Not only did it discredit the British army, but despoiling the countryside often lost the army many men who were picked off by enraged Americans.

The closer André became to Clinton, the more he found to admire in his commander. Underneath his crust, Clinton was gentle, kind, and very much filled with self-doubt. None of this was visible to his soldiers or his officers, who saw only the gruff, snarling warrior. And as Clinton daily observed his young aide at work, he drew him more and more into his confidence. Clinton probably recognized but would not admit that John André was the intellectual superior of any general officer in the British forces in America, and he encouraged André to offer him advice on military strategy where he would have dressed down any other officer who dared make such impertinent suggestions.

Perhaps the key to André's success in getting close to the austere Clinton was his mastery of psychology. André let Clinton know that he could confide in the younger officer and what he said would go no further. Clinton also knew that when he accepted André's advice, his aide would not brag about it to his fellow officers, but would instead credit the glory to Clinton.

André was the prototype of the perfect secretary, who intercepted all business requiring the general's signature or approval, agreeing to press those matters which he thought Clinton should pay attention to and dismissing those which he regarded as too trivial for the commander in chief's attention.

In this manner, John André obliged everyone in the British army who had business with Clinton to see him first. André once again gained a reputation as an aide who, if he agreed to present a person's petition to Clinton, would give the petitioner an answer within twenty-four hours.

André's special relationship with Clinton gave him a subtle but very real power in the General officers who previously had issued peremptory orders to the ambitious young captain were now forced to couch their requests in polite tones if they wanted them ever to reach Clinton's ear. André assumed the mantle of power with ease, as though born to command. On Clinton's behalf, he issued orders to his military superiors, occasionally inserting phrases like "the commander-in-chief has asked me to direct you . . ."

Thus it was that André could negotiate directly with Arnold on Clinton's behalf, a fact that Arnold was to find galling, especially when the British major didn't seem too excited about the prospect of Benedict Arnold's making a magnificently dramatic change of sides. Arnold would have to come with a dowry of troops or an important post, and Sir Henry, speaking through André, was not nearly as eager as Arnold to set a price for the American's defection or to establish a per-capita fee for the number of

American soldiers Arnold delivered into British hands at the time of his departure.

On May 23, Arnold wrote to André, "I cannot promise success; I will deserve it." (When Washington wrote to Arnold in Canada, he told him, "It is not in the power of any man to command success, but you have done more; you have deserved it.")

To demonstrate his ability to supply the British with valuable information, Arnold threw in a few facts about troop and naval movements, none of which impressed British headquarters enough to even take note of them.

Arnold did not hear from André again until June, for André was busy assisting Sir Henry Clinton in his lightning attack up the Hudson on the fortifications at Stony Point and Verplanck's Landing on the other side of what was known as King's Ferry, perhaps the narrowest section of the Hudson south of West Point. It was this thrust of British power that caused the final delay of Arnold's court-martial until the conclusion of the summer campaign.

When André replied, he suggested that Arnold rejoin the army, secure a command, then permit himself to be surprised and cut off, with five or six thousand men falling into British hands.

André also suggested that the two of them meet to iron out all remaining details and that meanwhile Arnold could busy himself with trying to secure the exchange of Burgoyne's army, which had been held in captivity, contrary to the terms of the surrender, by a Congress which chose to ignore treaties and agreements whenever it could. André hinted that the hero of Saratoga was perhaps the best man to achieve this humanitarian object.

André's concern for the fate of the Saratoga victims has a personal aspect to it, for few British officers had undergone the humiliation and degradation suffered by André when he was a captive of the Americans. But it is unpleasantly true that American prisoners who did not enjoy the rank of officers were treated abysmally by the British, who threw them into the infamous prison ships that rocked in the tides of New York Bay off Brooklyn and in the Hudson River off southern Manhattan. Neither side during the Revolution was humane in its treatment of prisoners, but the British probably won when it came to the number of their prisoners who died of starvation, mulnutrition, and disease in the holds of the wretched prison ships.

Benedict Arnold, who was risking his neck in an effort to join the British and bring the American Revolution to a speedy conclusion, was not pleased with the attitude of the British headquarters staff. They were treating his magnificent offer as an ordinary petition from a common soldier, and Arnold was not about to tolerate such treatment.

Following André's letter, Arnold dashed off a note explaining that he had "carefully examined the letter and found by the laconic style and little attention paid to my request that the gentleman [Major André] appeared very indifferent respecting the matter."

Arnold was infuriated that his gesture should meet with contempt, an insult he had too often experienced from his American colleagues. The greatest warrior of the age should be rewarded with gold and titles, and here he was being snubbed by both sides.

Stansbury, sensing that all was not well between his

two correspondents, directly informed André that his most recent letter "is not equal to his [Arnold's] expectations. He expects to have your promise that he shall be indemnified against any loss he may sustain in case of detection and whether this contest is finished by sword or treaty; that ten thousand pounds shall be engaged him for his services, which shall be faithfully devoted to your interests."

André took his time replying, waiting until the end of July before he wrote Stansbury that Arnold's demands required some heavy thinking at British headquarters. This was probably a ruse to stall Arnold until André and Clinton could get together and resolve between them how much Arnold's defection would be worth to the British cause. Here was a hero for sale, but his value on the international marketplace could not as yet be determined, and the British high command wanted to wait until they could bargain realistically for Arnold's services.

André wrote Arnold that if he could obtain a command and confer with André—if only for a few minutes—the details could be worked out. "Permit me to prescribe a little exertion. It is the procuring an accurate plan of West Point . . ."

The dice had been rolled, and André was the roller. Nothing had previously been said about West Point, but at this moment it is not hard to see the workings of the minds of Clinton and André. If Arnold could secure the command of West Point and weaken it for a successful British attack, it might be possible for the British to gain control of the upper Hudson and thus effectively split the rebel colonies in two.

André's letter to Arnold is at the same time bold,

demanding, reassuring, and flattering. In addition to asking for a detailed plan of West Point, André also requested "an account of what vessels, gunboats or galleys are in the North [Hudson] River or may be shortly built there, and the weight of metal they carry . . . sketches or descriptions of harbors to the eastward which might be attacked and where stores and shipping might be destroyed."

After suggesting that Arnold assume a command, André persuasively pointed out that a personal meeting

would satisfy you entirely and I trust would give us equal cause to be pleased. . . . But above all, Sir, let us not lose time or contract our views which on our part have become sanguine from the extensive strain of your overtures, and which we cannot think you would on your side confine to general intelligence whilst so much greater things may be done and advantages in proportion as much greater can be reaped.

Arnold did not reply directly to this letter, but showed it to Stansbury and salted the air with some strong remarks, judging by Stansbury's undated letter to André, written in code, based this time on Bailey's *Dictionary*, 23rd edition.

Arnold, Stansbury reported, noted that André's letter

contained no reply to the terms mentioned in my last [letter]. Though he could not doubt your honor yet there was no assurance given that his property in this country should be indemnified from any loss that might attend unfortunate discovery; however sincerely he wished to serve hs country in accellerating the settlement of this unhappy contest [the war], yet he should hold himself unjust to his family to hazard his all on the occasion and part with a certainty (potential at least) for an uncertainty. He hopes to join the army in about 3 weeks when he will, if possible, contrive an interview.

Stansbury continues at some length with trivial military intelligence Arnold had supplied, pointing out that only Washington and his engineers had access to the complete plans of West Point, but once Arnold was there he could send back more detailed information.

At the end of this letter, Stansbury gives us a brief glimpse of his own personality.

"I am sensible I have been tedious and have not leisure at this late hour to throw it into better order or smaller compass. Saturday 3 AM."

It is easy to imagine this dapper young china dealer lighting candle after candle through the night as he labored over this coded letter, playing his unheralded role in a conspiracy that would erupt in America like a volcano. The drudgery and leg work of the conspiracy were conducted by Joseph Stansbury and Jonathan Odell, yet their names would be all but lost in a history that concerned itself with the villainy of Benedict Arnold and the noble self-sacrifice of John André. Yet without Odell's connections with André and the British general staff and Stansbury's willingness to risk his neck time and again to deliver and convey messages, the great conspiracy could have gone nowhere. A parson without a congregation and a Philadelphia storekeeper are the supporting characters in this tragedy, and without them there would have been no drama.

At this point in the conspiracy, negotiations came to a standstill, with Arnold demanding a written guarantee of $10,000 for changing his allegiance and $20,000 for the successful delivery of West Point into British hands. The British were reluctant to set a specific figure until after they were positive that they were indeed dealing with Benedict Arnold and not some clever American double agent who was luring them into a trap.

The fact that Arnold did not return to the army increased British suspicions. André decided to try his hand with Peggy, whom he addressed directly on August 16, 1779, with an offer to become her New York milliner. "I shall be glad to enter into the whole detail of capwire, needles, gauze, etc., and, to the best of my abilities, render you in these trifles services from which I hope you would infer a zeal to be further employed."

This elegant prose, when translated into the thoughts of Peggy and André, is a clear offer to resume the negotiations, perhaps via Peggy. But Mistress Arnold waited a good two months before she politely replied to Captain André that another officer "was so obliging as to promise to procure what trifles Mrs. Arnold wanted in the millinery way, or she would with pleasure have accepted of it [André's offer]. Mrs. Arnold begs leave to assure Capt. André that her friendship and esteem for him is not impaired by time or accident."

Translation: until the British answer her husband's financial requirements with solid guarantees, Peggy told André, he need not bother with any more negotiations.

There is a curious aspect about Benedict Arnold which surfaces from time to time during the seventeen months between his first message to André and the climax of the conspiracy. That is that Arnold had made up his mind to defect to the British, but he seemed to be looking for a chance to back out and resume fighting for the American cause. He knew that he was compromised with the British and that they could destroy him by revealing his part in the conspiracy to the Americans. However, if Arnold had won recognition by Congress for his efforts and if the Pennsylvania council dropped its accusations against him and if he were offered a field command in time, he could withdraw from the British deal and, should the details be made public, could explain in advance to Washington that this had been a ruse of his to get intelligence from the British and pretend to cooperate with them in order to trap and destroy Clinton's army.

At any rate, both Arnold and André had pressing matters which required their attention to the point where negotiations would not resume in earnest until the spring of 1780. By that time, Arnold had been court-martialed; André had assisted Clinton in the successful siege of Charleston, South Carolina; the American army had undergone its most severe winter encampment at Morristown, New Jersey; Congress was riddled with corruption; and American morale was at its lowest ebb.

Arnold's wounded leg continued to throb unpleasantly, often to the point where he had to be assisted in and out of his carriage by as many as four aides. And when that leg was not acting up, gout was making its earliest appearance in his other leg.

Despite the official reprimand Washington had been obliged to deliver to Arnold, the commander in chief still regarded the embattled little Connecticut gamecock as his best general. As the snow melted and the dogwoods blossomed in Morristown, Washington drew up plans for his coming campaign.

He would command the center of the army, while Nathanael Greene would be given charge of the right wing. But the left wing—the position of honor which would include command of the cavalry and the light infantry—Washington resolved to bestow on the one man who deserved it most, Benedict Arnold.

Washington himself may not have been a very good general, and military historians tend to rate him rather low as a strategist, but he recognized talent with an unerring eye. Once Congress stopped interfering in the appointment of generals, Washington was able to dispatch excellent commanders such as Nathanael Greene and Anthony Wayne in ways that would ultimately win the Revolution.

His selection of Arnold to command the left wing was brilliant. But it was too late.

II. The Conspiracy Blossoms

DURING THE early months of 1780, Benedict Arnold made one last gesture before committing himself irrevocably to the British. Already reprimanded by a court-martial and denied payment in full of his expenses by Congress, Arnold wrote Washington that he had heard that the admiralty board was making plans for a Continental navy. Arnold asked Washington's endorsement to take charge of the navy. "From the injury I have received in my leg and the great stiffness in my ankle, my surgeons are of the opinion it will not be prudent for me to take a command in the army for some time to come." However, an admiral need not mount a bucking horse and gallop into battle, but instead can direct naval maneuvers from an armchair.

Washington passed on Arnold's request to Congress, noting that he had no authority over such matters. Nothing came of the projected fleet or the expedition against British shipping, but for a few days we can see Benedict Arnold recalling the seagoing days of his youth and the excitement of sighting the cannons as his pathetic little fleet held the mighty British navy at bay one crisp October afternoon on Lake Champlain. The roar of the cannon is a sound that fades very slowly from one's memory.

Early in March of 1780, while Arnold was still brooding and wondering whether to reopen the negotiations, an old friend, General Philip Schuyler, arrived in Philadelphia, this time as a representative to Congress from the State of New York. Schuyler was shortly appointed chairman of a congressional committee to meet with Washington in his Morristown headquarters in the Ford Mansion, to discuss organization of the army and incorporating the French troops into the existing units.

But before Schuyler left Philadelphia, he and Arnold must have chatted at some length about the chunky general's future, for on May 25 Arnold wrote to Schuyler in Morristown that "I have not had the pleasure of receiving a line from you since you arrived at camp, and know not who is to have the command at the North River."

Command of the North, or Hudson, River meant not only West Point but all the fortifications along it. Writing a letter he hoped Schuyler would show Washington, Arnold continued:

When I requested leave of absence of his Excellency General Washington for the summer, it was under the idea that it would be a very inactive campaign and that my services would be of little consequence, as my wounds made it very painful for me to walk or ride. The prospect now seems to be altered, and there is a probability of an active campaign; in which, though attended with pain and difficulty, I wish to render my country every service in my power, and with the advice of my friends am determined to join the army; of which I beg you will do me the favor to acquaint his Excellency George Washington that I may be included in any arrangement that may be made.

Schuyler did exactly as Arnold hoped he would, and showed the letter to Washington. Writing to Arnold, Schuyler described how

. . . I had conversed with the general on the subject which passed between us before I left Philadelphia; that he appeared undecided on the occasion, I believe because no arrangement was made, for he expressed himself with regard to you in terms such as the friends who love you could wish.

When I received yours of the 25th May, I read it to him. He was much engaged; next day he requested to know the contents again. I put it onto his hands. He expressed a desire to do whatever was agreeable to you, dwelt on your abilities, your merits, your sufferings, and on the well-earned claims you have on your country, and intimated that as soon as his arrangements for the campaign should take place that he would properly consider you. I believe you will have an alternative proposed, either in charge of an important post, with an honorable command, or your station in the field. Your reputation, my dear sir, so established, your honorable scars, put it decidedly in your power to take either. A state [New York] which has full confidence in you will wish to see its banner entrusted to you. If the command at West Point is offered, it will be honorable; if a division in the field, you must judge whether you can support the fatigues, circumstanced as you are.

Events in the conspiracy now move swiftly. Having hinted to Washington through the innocent Schuyler that he wanted command of West Point, Arnold assumed that it was his, and he reopened negotiations with the British to discuss the best possible way to hand it over to them. His first letters were received by a bewildered General Wilhelm von Knyphausen, who was minding the store in New York while Clinton and André were busy capturing Charleston. When they returned to New York, however, they both studied Arnold's letters closely and decided that the time to act had arrived.

Arnold visited Washington in Morristown on June 12, conferred with him, and immediately passed on to the British the news that the French fleet was planning to land at Newport and then attack Canada, a phony story that

Washington was spreading in the hope that it would lure
Clinton away from New York long enough for him to
attack and capture the island city. Arnold traveled from
Morristown to Connecticut, where he made arrangements
to sell his house and property. He then rode over to West
Point for the first time, and, in the company of a genial
colleague, General Robert Howe, inspected its defenses. To
Howe, Arnold was severe in his criticism of its fortifications, mentally noting how he could further weaken Washington's precious citadel of the north.

On July 31, Washington moved his troops across the
Hudson at King's Ferry near Stony Point, when he met
Arnold in a fateful session.

The only first-person account of that meeting—other
than various letters Arnold wrote to the British indicating
that the West Point command was his—is Washington's
own recollection, recorded by his private secretary, Tobias
Lear, in 1786, six years after the incident.

While the army was crossing at King's Ferry, I was going
to see the last detachment over and met Arnold, who asked
me if I had thought of anything. I told him that he was to
have command of the light troops, which was a post of
honor and which his rank indeed entitled him to. [Most historians agree that Washington's memory failed him in this
recollection and that he rather offered Arnold command of
the left wing, a position commensurate with Arnold's rank and
talent, which would have included the light troops.]
Upon this information his countenance changed, and he
appeared to be quite fallen; and instead of thanking me, or
expressing any pleasure at the appointment, never opened his
mouth.

Upon his return to headquarters, and after discovering
that Clinton had changed his plans and decided against an
attack on the French in Rhode Island, Washington decided

that while it would be a waste of an excellent field officer, he could not refuse Arnold's request. "I then determined to comply with Arnold's desire, and accordingly gave him the command of the garrison at West Point."

The chill that went through Arnold at Washington's magnanimous offer—which came just a bit too late—was probably equaled by the puzzlement besetting the commander in chief when his fire-eating, scrappy field genius turned down the choicest plum of command in favor of a dull administrative job in a remote fort.

Arnold had left Philadelphia several days before his meeting with Washington, confident that the West Point command was his. Before leaving, he dropped various hints to the British that he was enroute to prepare for his involvement in the conspiracy, hoping to force the British finally to agree to his financial demands. He also decided to cover his tracks by asking Congress on July 17 for an advance against his salary (unpaid for four years) of $25,000 with which to purchase field equipment. In his first meeting with Washington following the reprimand, Arnold indicated his desire to rejoin the army, but first hinted about West Point. Washington, who was greatly embarrassed by what he had been forced to write to Arnold, readily countersigned Arnold's request for a salary advance, a factor which undoubtedly sped it through the congressional committees.

Although Arnold's appointment to head the left wing was published in the general orders from Peekskill on August 1, Washington corrected it, and on August 3 it was announced that Arnold would take command of West Point, enabling General Robert Howe to return to the American line.

By August 5, Howe had packed up and left, while Arnold took possession of the West Point commander's official residence, a large house on the other side of the river from the fort and approximately two miles away. This house had belonged to the Tory Colonel Beverley Robinson, a wealthy landowner in the Hudson Valley and an old friend of George Washington's.

Arnold quickly set about to resolve the conspiracy as rapidly as possible. He sent for Peggy and their baby son, Edward, while he supplemented his official family with aides Major David Franks and Lieutenant Colonel Richard Varick, both of whom he heavily involved in his scheme for handing over West Point without giving them the least hint of his double-dealing.

Arnold had settled in when a letter from André reached him on August 24, indicating that the British would meet Arnold's financial demands and pay him £20,000 when he surrendered West Point, all its stores and artillery, and a garrison in the neighborhood of 3,000 men.

It has been generally assumed in popular histories that Arnold promptly set out to weaken West Point by draining its garrison and neglecting its defenses. Since there was always a chance that the plot might go awry, Arnold actually was scrupulous in pointing out to Howe and Washington (and to the British) the weak points in the fortifications, places where an aggressive enemy could batter its way into the inner defenses. Rather than decimate the garrison, Arnold knew that he had to fatten the numbers to at least 3,000 men in order to meet Clinton's requirements for payment in full. His theory seemed to be that if he spread his troops out in isolated clusters, they could better be surprised and captured.

Proponents of the theory that Arnold was deliberately weakening the fort point to his order for 200 men to move north to Fishkill to chop enough wood for the garrison during the winter. Arnold's old friend, Colonel John Lamb, now commander of artillery at West Point, protested loudly to Arnold—Arnold would take disagreement from a friend like Lamb—that if he kept up this drain of men from the main garrison, "we shall neither be able to finish the works that are incomplete nor be in a situation to defend those that are finished."

This quote has been trotted out time and again to show how Lamb saw through Arnold's ruse. However, what is rarely pointed out is that Arnold had already asked for, and received, permission from General Washington for this expedition.

During the ensuing weeks, Arnold behaved properly as an American general, so as not to attract any attention as a potential defector. Instead of trying to weaken the massive iron chain stretched across the river from West Point to the other side, Arnold reported to Washington that he would strengthen it in accord with an engineer's recommendation, but that he could not get the necessary materials.

One of his first steps was to ask Lafayette for the names of his spies among the British in New York, and Howe for a list of his spies and couriers. Both men turned him down simply because the agents they worked with refused to let their names be divulged to anyone, preferring to remain known only to the one man they dealt with.

Also around this time, Lafayette's spies in New York were picking up rumors of an impending defection of someone high in the American command. Since these rumors frequently floated around, little attention was paid to them. Those officers who tried to sniff out potential traitors among the Americans never thought about Arnold, so apparently unswerving was his loyalty.

Meanwhile, Arnold found that getting word to and from the British was much more difficult at West Point than at Philadelphia. He finally got word to the British, as Varick later reported, pretending to be contacting "a person in New York whose fictitious name was John Anderson, to establish a line of intelligence of the enemy's movements."

Arnold suggested that André try to enter the American lines in disguise in order that the two of them might confer in secret regarding the precise timetable for the British assault on West Point. Clinton was adamant that no aide of his—and André had just been promoted to the post of adjutant general—should sneak into enemy lines like a common spy.

Arnold had paved the way for André to slip inside the lines by writing to Colonel Elisha Sheldon, then commander of a band of cavalry near Salem, and the outpost commander at North Castle, Major Benjamin Tallmadge, requesting their cooperation and assistance should a man named John Anderson enter their lines.

Meanwhile, a meeting was arranged by Arnold for September 11 at Dobbs Ferry, on the east bank of the Hudson. Arnold had himself rowed in his barge to within less than a mile of Dobbs Ferry, when a gunboat from the British sloop of war *Vulture*—the navy not having been apprised of the army's plan—started firing at Arnold's barge, forcing it to the west shore. Directly across the river from him stood Major André and Colonel Robinson. Both parties waited for the other to cross the river under a flag of truce, but neither would make the first move. Arnold was hemmed in at the little cove at Sneden's Landing by the prowling British gunboat, which seemed to be daring him to sail out into the river. And on the other bank, André and Robinson sat on their horses, watching their efforts being defeated by their own navy. André had already won Sir Henry's reluctant permission to meet with Arnold, and it was probably during this aborted attempt that the young aide decided to set a new date and board the *Vulture*, where Arnold could come under a flag of truce.

Arnold returned to the Robinson house, from where he wrote André on September 15. He proposed to send a local suspected Tory, Joshua Hett Smith—whom the members of Arnold's military family detested—to meet André at Dobbs Ferry on the night of September 20, "who will conduct you to a place of safety, where I will meet you. It will be necessary for you to be disguised . . ."

Shortly after dispatching this letter, Arnold received one from Washington revealing that he would be at Peekskill the following Sunday night (September 17), on his way to Hartford to confer with the French admiral and general, and requesting Arnold to send along a guard of a captain and fifty men, together with a night's forage to feed forty horses.

"You will keep this to yourself, as I want to make my journey a secret," Washington concluded, addressing the wrong man. Arnold promptly communicated this intelligence to André, along with the suggestion that a fast

British expedition could surprise the Americans, capture Washington, and very likely win the war. (The British failed to take advantage of this unusual opportunity.)

After writing André for a second time, Arnold hurried across the river to Joshua Smith's house, perched atop a hill on the west bank of the Hudson outside of Haverstraw where his beloved Peggy had finally arrived with their baby son.

The following Sunday, Arnold, Peggy, Varick, Franks, and Lamb were dining at the Robinson house when a messenger arrived with a letter for Arnold from the owner of the house, Colonel Beverley Robinson, who was at that moment aboard His Majesty's sloop of war *Vulture*, anchored off Teller's Point. As part of the plot, Robinson requested an interview with Aronld, but Lamb protested heatedly that such requests should only be directed to the civilian authorities of the state. Arnold later asked Washington, who concurred. So Arnold dictated a stiff rejection of Robinson's request to Varick.

Along with the official letter to Robinson, Arnold enclosed a secret message that he would send a messenger to the *Vulture* on the night of the twentieth, there to pick up André, disguised as John Anderson, for a trip inside the American lines.

To Smith, who never really knew what Arnold was up to, Arnold issued a pass authorizing him to bring John Anderson from the sloop to Smith's house. Arnold forestalled Smith's suspicions by assuring him that Anderson was really Colonel Robinson or one of his colleagues coming to present favorable peace terms to the Americans.

A study of the correspondence between Arnold and André makes it clear that Arnold expected André to take all the risks of disguising himself and slipping through the American lines.

But Sir Henry Clinton read the messages differently: André would go ashore under a flag of truce and meet with Arnold outside either army's lines. It is possible that in his exuberance to conclude the exciting business, André neglected to show Clinton all of Arnold's correspondence, possibly paraphrasing it for him, omitting the stipulations about disguise and entering the American lines.

Clinton was genuinely fond of the young adjutant general, and he couldn't help smiling at the boy's determination to personally conclude the plot he had masterminded from the start.

There is one legend about André's final session with Clinton which deserves to be repeated, true or not. After the injunction against removing his regimentals, entering the enemy lines, or carrying any incriminating evidence, all of which André solemnly promised, Clinton is said to have walked over to a sideboard by the fireplace in his office, picked up a decanter of claret, poured out two glasses, handed one to André, and raised his own in a toast.

"Here's to plain John André. May he return Sir John André."

12. The Meeting in the Firs

ANDRÉ GALLOPED ACROSS King's Bridge (connecting Manhattan with Westchester) and north to Dobbs Ferry, his cloak flying behind him and his scarlet and white regimentals glowing in the moonlight. There he was taken by boat out to the *Vulture*, where he met Robinson and conferred with the ship's captain, Andrew Sutherland. It is doubtful whether he told Sutherland his mission, but he apparently impressed him with its secrecy, for Sutherland does not mention either his arrival or Robinson's in the ship's log.

André paced the deck restlessly, waiting for Arnold's representative, but none showed up and he was forced to retire for the night. What had happened was that Joshua Smith had been unable to persuade a local boatman to take him out to the *Vulture* that night.

The next morning André wrote somewhat agitatedly to Clinton, "This is the second excursion I have made without ostensible reason, and Colonel Robinson both times of the party. A third would infallibly fix suspicions."

In order to keep the crew from speculating about the continued presence of the adjutant general on board, André sent a second letter—which he made sure the officers and crew heard about—saying that he had "caught a very bad cold and so violent a return of the disorder in my stomach" that he wished to remain on board until he could comfortably return to New York.

Meanwhile, he and Robinson sat down together to prepare a note to Arnold, over Robinson's signature but in André's own hand—which he expected Arnold to recognize immediately—protesting the American violation of the code of war by firing on a flag of truce sent out with one of the *Vulture*'s boats a few days earlier. This letter was sent under a flag of truce to Arnold, who was already well on his way toward the *Vulture*, using an inspection of his fortifications as an excuse. Arnold conferred with Colonel James Livingston, who was in command of the section of the Hudson from Verplanck's Point to Teller's Point.

Livingston considered the presence of the *Vulture* off Teller's Point an impudence which should be challenged by a cannonade from the unfortified promontory of land. Livingston had applied to his superior, Lamb, for permission to shell the *Vulture*, and Lamb, though certain that the ship was too far out to be hit by any American artillery, gave Livingston his permission to go ahead and try. Arnold was unaware of this development as he prepared to send Smith to the ship that night to bring André over to the west shore of Haverstraw Bay, where there was a stand of firs which would adequately conceal them.

When Arnold arrived at Smith's house, he found that the two boatmen, Samuel and Joseph Colquehoun, didn't want to row out to the ship. These two, who appear from contemporary descriptions to have been borderline imbeciles, were in awe of General Arnold, but not so much that they would exercise their rowing muscles after working hard all day. Arnold was at first patient with them, appealing to their patriotism. When his charm and persuasive rhetoric failed, Arnold's famous temper flared, and he threatened to imprison them at once as British sympathizers. They agreed to row.

Arnold then wrote out a pass for Smith and the boatmen, and handed Smith a letter to deliver personally to Robinson.

This will be delivered to you by Mr. Smith who will conduct you to a place of safety. Neither Mr. Smith nor any other person shall be acquainted with your proposals. If they (which I doubt not) are of such a nature that I can officially take notice of them, I shall do it with pleasure. If not, you shall be permitted to return immediately. I take it for granted Colonel Robinson will not propose anything that is not for the interest of the United States as well as himself.

The letter itself was a ruse to get Smith past any suspicious guards, but Arnold had no intention of meeting with Beverley Robinson. Along with the letter he had added a scrap of paper with the simple scribble, "Gustavus to John Anderson."

Smith climbed on board the *Vulture* and was ushered immediately into Sutherland's cabin. He undoubtedly recognized Beverley Robinson and exchanged some pleasantries with him while André—in another cabin—read Arnold's letter and noted with satisfaction the scrap of paper.

Smith returned to the deck while André, Sutherland, and Robinson held a last-minute conference. There was no question that André was the man to go ashore, but Sutherland suggested that it might be safer if he were to

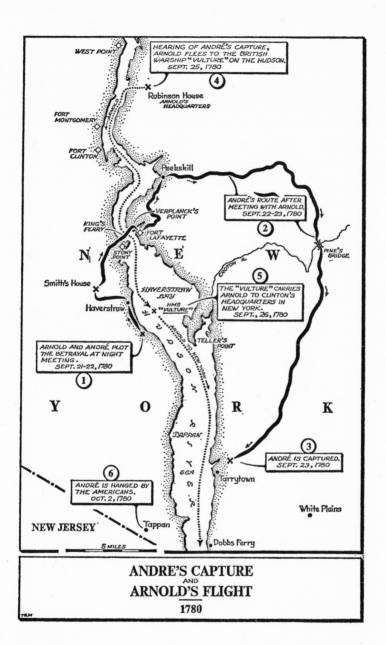

WEST POINT

HEARING OF ANDRÉ'S CAPTURE, ARNOLD FLEES TO THE BRITISH WARSHIP "VULTURE" ON THE HUDSON. SEPT. 25, 1780 ④

Robinson House *ARNOLD'S HEADQUARTERS*

FORT MONTGOMERY

FORT CLINTON

Peekskill

VERPLANCK'S POINT

KING'S FERRY

FORT LAFAYETTE

ANDRÉ'S ROUTE AFTER MEETING WITH ARNOLD. SEPT. 22-23, 1780 ②

PINE'S BRIDGE

N

E

CROTON R.

W

STONY POINT

THE "VULTURE" CARRIES ARNOLD TO CLINTON'S HEADQUARTERS IN NEW YORK. SEPT., 1780 ⑤

Smith's House

HAVERSTRAW BAY

HMS "VULTURE"

Haverstraw

TELLER'S POINT

ARNOLD AND ANDRÉ PLOT THE BETRAYAL AT NIGHT MEETING. SEPT. 21-22, 1780 ①

ARNOLD TO NEW YORK

Y   O   R   K

HUDSON R.

TAPPAN SEA

ANDRÉ IS CAPTURED. SEPT. 23, 1780 ③

Tarrytown

White Plains

ANDRÉ IS HANGED BY THE AMERICANS. OCT. 2, 1780 ⑥

NEW JERSEY   Tappan

Dobbs Ferry

5 MILES

ANDRE'S CAPTURE
AND
ARNOLD'S FLIGHT
1780

TRM

don less conspicuous clothes. Recalling the admonitions of Sir Henry, André insisted that he must go ashore as a British officer. But supposing an American patrol boat spotted his scarlet regimentals and took a shot at him? André finally agreed to wear a large blue coat over his uniform. But shouldn't Robinson accompany him, just to be safe? The passes made out by Arnold covered only one man to return with Smith.

"Major André thought it was best for him to go alone," Robinson wrote Clinton, since "it appeared to him, as indeed it did to me, that Arnold wished to see him."

Robinson led André onto the deck and presented him to Smith as Mr. John Anderson, who would represent Robinson in a conference with Arnold. Smith couldn't have cared less whom he accompanied to meet with Arnold, since he was merely doing yet another favor for the general who had honored him with his friendship and protection.

The boat rowed two miles from the ship to a prearranged spot on the shore, a pile of rocks forming a natural landing place and known ever since as André's Dock. It was a moonlit night, and André took advantage of the boat trip and Smith's silence to quickly sketch the scene of the little rowboat pulling toward the shore, with High Tor unmistakable in the background. This would be a pleasant little memento of his adventure.

At this point, it should be noted that while André was complying with the letter of Clinton's orders by not removing his regimentals, he had indeed covered them. Also, it seems to have been fully understood by everyone involved (except Clinton) that if their business was not concluded before daybreak, André and Arnold would retire to Smith's house, there to await nightfall and the adjutant general's return to the ship by boat. André needed no map of the Haverstraw area to know that Smith's house was well within the American lines, and that to reach it, he and Arnold would have to pass American sentries. This was the first step toward André's self-incrimination as a spy.

Of course, there was no doubt in André's mind that he would return to the *Vulture*—if all went well, that night—but if not, he would be perfectly safe in Smith's house. He was reasonably certain that he and Arnold could thresh out the details of the attack on West Point, timing it to perfection. Since financial matters had been agreed upon by letter, the conversation would be principally military.

And even if he did spend the day inside the rebel lines, it would make his exploits that much more heroic when his role in crushing the American Revolution became known. If by his own genius, daring, charm, and military brilliance, John André could lead the way to a total British victory in America, he would share in the laurels with Sir Henry and Arnold. A knighthood was the least of his prospects. More likely, a generalship and possibly even a dukedom.

It is ironic that André's entire plan hinged—for just an hour or two—on the whim of the Colquehoun brothers. These two successfully ruined the entire conspiracy and probably changed the course of American history by their indolence and blockheaded refusal to row André back to the *Vulture*.

But this is jumping the sequence by twenty-four hours, a day when the entire war hung delicately in the hands of a few men.

These same Colquehoun brothers were putting their backs to the chore of rowing across the Hudson as André finished his sketch. Smith, who had been at the rudder, glanced occasionally at his companion, who appeared to be an unusually handsome youth, perhaps a British subaltern who wanted to defect to the Americans. Neither Smith nor André recalled their having dined together five years earlier, when André had been a prisoner of war on his way to internment in Pennsylvania and only an insignificant lieutenant.

From the moment Major André stepped ashore until Smith informed Arnold at 4:00 A.M. that dawn was rapidly approaching, there is no accurate history except Smith's accounts. Since he told one story while on trial for his life by the Americans, who accused him of complicity with Arnold in the conspiracy, and another years later when he was trying to convince the British government of his loyalty to the Crown, there is some reason to doubt his accuracy, not to mention his strict adherence to the truth.

Smith is probably telling the truth when he describes how he told "Mr Anderson" to wait on the shore while he scrambled into the mass of evergreens where Arnold was waiting. Smith breathlessly told Arnold that Colonel Robinson had refused to come ashore, but had sent as his representative a man called John Anderson. Continuing to play his role, Arnold grumbled at Robinson's balkiness, then casually told Smith that since Anderson had gone to the trouble of coming ashore, he might as well meet with him.

Smith went back to André and pointed him in the right direction. There, in the darkness of the forest, the adjutant general of the British army saluted the hero of Saratoga. The two men shook hands, and what happened the rest of that night is one of history's darkest secrets.

13. André in Flight

WHEN Joshua Hett Smith informed Arnold and André at 4:00 A.M., during their meeting in the firs, that dawn was approaching, their business apparently was far from concluded, for Arnold ordered up a spare horse to convey André with him to Smith's house. André was evidently satisfied at the progress of their session and was anxious to continue the negotiations, perhaps in the safety of Smith's house, even though it lay well within the American lines. After all, Arnold had assured him that once night fell, the Colquehoun brothers would row him back to the *Vulture*.

André was tired, but filled with the excitement of his mission. He and Arnold had covered some major points, including Arnold's compensation, as dawn broke over the Hudson. But there were so many little details to work out about how the British could successfully storm West Point that André wanted to get every one down in his memory, since he would no doubt be leading one column of the attack force.

Thus, Arnold's suggestion that they adjourn to Smith's house for the remainder of the morning made eminent sense, and André did not balk when a horse was led out of the forest to convey him to Haverstraw.

Once ensconced in the Smith house—Joshua had conveniently moved his family to Fishkill for a vacation—

André and Arnold concluded their negotiations. As André was preparing to get some sleep before he returned to his ship that night, the two conspirators were startled by the sound of cannon coming from the river. It seems that Colonel Livingston, having received Lamb's permission to shell the *Vulture*, had dragged cannon and howitzers to the top of Teller's Point, and at sunrise proceeded to raise merry hell with His Majesty's sloop of war. Despite Lamb's laughing denial that a battery on Teller's Point could bother the British ship, Livingston, with perhaps a few glasses of rum aboard, was determined to make the British jump, and he was successful. His heavy cannonade blistered the sloop so badly that Sutherland, swearing mightily, let slip the anchor and dropped downstream several hundred yards. The sails were torn by cannon shot, and one of the balls hit the deck, throwing a splinter into Captain Sutherland's nose.

André and Arnold, watching from the windows of Smith's house, saw the *Vulture* slip anchor and move downstream. André knew that it would be just far enough to stay out of cannon range, but Arnold was afraid the sloop might return to New York.

To protect his confidant, Arnold issued two sets of passes to Smith, one to allow André to return as he came, by boat, to the *Vulture*, the other to cover an overland journey through Westchester should a return to the boat be impossible. The latter course, André informed Arnold, was unthinkable, since he was still a British officer in uniform. Arnold may have cynically replied that he could wear his uniform right past the sentries if he wished, but it would not help him get back to Sir Henry safely.

It is customary at this point for historians to draw the

sharp contrast between the handsome young adjutant general of the British army and the corrupt major general who was in the process of betraying his country to the enemy. There is no question that John André was a sparkling young British officer, but there also is no question that Benedict Arnold was still the most dashing, heroic figure in the Continental army. It is true that Arnold was deeply involved in a plot to overthrow Congress and return the colonies to British rule, but for his sake we must remember that he regarded himself in the same light as General Monk. Had he succeeded, none would have dared call it treason.

Both were short men, yet both overrode this physical handicap. Arnold was thirty-nine, while André was ten years his junior.

We know nothing of what either man thought about the other during their memorable meeting. It is possible that Arnold paid less attention to the suave young British major than he should have, for André was, in fact, an officer of inferior grade whom Arnold shortly would be commanding. And Arnold did not see sharing his glory with anyone else. He could not imagine the personal involvement in the plot of men such as André and Clinton, Stansbury and Odell. He, Benedict Arnold, was the war hero who was taking the dramatic—and potentially disastrous—step of transferring his allegiance at the low point of the American Revolution.

André's opinion of Arnold at this moment is unrecorded, but we know that he shared with Clinton the excitement of finally luring to the British side a rebel general whose name was known on both continents.

After giving André the necessary passes and urging

him to change into civilian clothes should he be forced to travel overland—a possibility that André still dismissed—Arnold handed André a series of documents, including plans of West Point and top-secret minutes of a recent council of war presided over by General Washington.

Suggesting that André get some sleep before nightfall, Arnold said he had to return to West Point immediately lest his absence arouse suspicion. The two shook hands, never to meet again.

They had agreed that since the documents were in Arnold's undisguised handwriting, André should destroy them if he were intercepted on his way back to the ship. André agreed to attach them to a heavy stone and drop it overboard should such a surprise occur.

André was left in a second-floor bedroom while Smith accompanied Arnold on horseback to King's Ferry, where the General's barge was awaiting him. During their ride, Smith expressed some shock at seeing "Mr. Anderson" wearing the regimentals of a British staff officer. Arnold laughed nervously, pointing out that Mr. Anderson was a vain young merchant who, out of pride, had borrowed the coat from an officer friend. And he added that should André be obliged to return to New York overland, Smith must insist that André change his clothes in order to avoid capture. It seems that Arnold regarded either possible route of return as safe and left the decision in Smith's hands.

When Smith returned to the house, he found the young officer pacing about in the bedroom. Smith informed André that the Colquehoun brothers refused to row him back to the *Vulture*, and that he would have to return to New York overland. André protested vehemently, especially when the question of his removing his regimentals was raised, but he dared not arouse Smith's suspicions, so he reluctantly changed into a claret-colored coat and a round-brimmed hat.

The two set out at nightfall on horseback, with Smith gabbing cheerfully while André remained silent. As they neared King's Ferry alongside Stony Point—where André had negotiated the surrender of American troops not long before—Smith became even more garrulous, dropping hints to American officers that he was on serious business for Major General Arnold.

Boarding the longboat ferry, André went immediately to the stern, with his face turned away from the oarsmen, any one of whom could have been among the prisoners he had taken at Stony Point. Smith, however, continued to gabble with one and all. Reaching the other side, Smith insisted that he had to share a cup of grog with Colonel Livingston, the local commandant and the man whose cannonade had supplied Captain Sutherland with a splinter in his nose. André remained outside while Smith slapped Livingston on the back and clanked several toasts with him. Livingston finally insisted that Smith bring his fellow traveler in for a mug of grog, but some unusual bit of common sense made Smith refuse, so the two cantered southward.

André had hoped to ride all night to White Plains, which was inside the British lines, but his plans were thwarted when a patrol of rebel militia, headed by Captain Ebenezer Boyd, stopped them near Crompond and cross-examined Smith thoroughly on his mission. Smith told them that he was accompanying Mr. Anderson to White Plains to gather military intelligence for General Arnold. Smith asked the best route to take, and the officious Captain

Boyd suggested that they ride via North Castle, since the Tarrytown approach to White Plains was dominated by the pro-British "Cowboys"—a band of thugs whose pro-American counterparts were the "Skinners."

This piece of information delighted André, but he had to conceal his relief from both Smith and Boyd. The captain rather pointedly told them that if they continued their nocturnal journey, they would be asking for trouble, and insisted that they bed down for the night nearby. André was enraged at this delay, but controlled his temper and allowed Smith to lead him to a nearby farmhouse, where they were able to obtain the use of one bed for the night. Smith later reported that he was continually awakened by André's tossing and rolling about and sighing.

André was awake well before daybreak, and he hustled Smith out of bed so they could be on their way. Just before reaching Pine's Bridge, crossing the Croton River—the boundary of no man's land—the two stopped for breakfast, and Smith casually informed André that they would now be parting, for Smith had to return to Fishkill to pick up his family. Besides, Mr Anderson could easily find his way from that point. André, who had no money with him, borrowed a few dollars from Smith, who refused to take André's watch in payment, perhaps one of the few decent things Smith did during this entire episode.

The two shook hands at Pine's Bridge on Saturday morning, September 23, and André—perhaps relieved by the absence of the chatty Smith, proceeded south toward White Plains.

At one point, he was confronted with a fork in the road, one branch of which would take him directly to

White Plains, while the other would take him there via Tarrytown, supposedly populated by pro-British Americans. Whether André deliberately or accidentally took the wrong fork is not known, but that lovely autumn morning he headed southwest toward Tarrytown.

As he neared his sanctuary, André heard the pounding of hoofs and looked up to see a rebel officer approaching him. It was Colonel Samuel Webb of Connecticut, who had been captured by the British but was now on parole. Webb knew André well, and André recognized Webb immediately. Pulling his round-brimmed hat down over his face and slouching in his saddle like a merchant rather than a soldier, André successfully passed his enemy.

The following scene is one of the most melodramatic in American history, and were it presented as fiction or drama, readers and audiences would hoot at it. Yet this is what happened.

Major John André, disguised as John Anderson, merchant, and with plans of West Point stuffed in his boot, was riding pleasantly through a beautiful autumn morning nearing Tarrytown.

He was admiring the fall foliage and perhaps thinking of how beautiful America was and how he might like to retire to the colonies following a full and active service in His Majesty's army. There now appear on the scene three bandits—no other word can accurately describe them—who, in the words of John Hyde Preston, that morning "thugged their way into history."

They were John Paulding, Isaac Van Wart, and David Williams. Each is buried in a prominently marked grave, they are commemorated by a monument in Tarrytown, and

Congress ordered a special medal struck in their honor.
Yet they were three of the blackest villains of the era who
just happened to stop the right man at the right time.

These noble three were playing cards by a stream,
waiting for some wealthy-looking horseman to come along
in order to mug him—they were common highwaymen.

Seeing André approach the bridge, they took one
look at his polished boots and decided that they might as
well line their pockets once again. They sprang out onto
the road in front of his horse, Paulding waving a musket,
and ordered him to stop. They did not shout, "Stand and
deliver!"—the traditional cry of the English highwayman
—but they might well have. They were interested in
money, not glory or patriotism. As a matter of fact,
Paulding was wearing a British army coat which he had
liberated from a corpse during a recent campaign.

The moment he was challenged, André, whose nerves
were edgy, noticed Paulding's coat and breathed a sigh of
relief. He told them he was a British officer, at which they
revealed that he had fallen into enemy hands. André
promptly whipped out Arnold's pass and showed it to
them, but his statement about being a British officer made
the thugs view it with suspicion. They ordered André to
dismount, which he did reluctantly.

"Had he pulled out General Arnold's pass first," Paulding later said, "I should have let him go."

However, the three really didn't care about politics as
much as they yearned for loot, and they searched André
thoroughly. Not finding anything in his pockets, they
decided that he must have money or valuables hidden on
his person, so they ordered him to strip. André reportedly
invoked Arnold's name, then, when this drew little re-

sponse, offered them money if they would deliver him safely to New York. They considered this, but decided that if they did take him to New York in hope of getting a ransom, André might send out British troops to arrest and hang them. So they continued their search.

The papers in André's stocking sealed his fate, for the moment they discovered these, Paulding, Van Wart, and Williams suddenly became patriots and promptly delivered André to Colonel John Jameson, who had relieved Colonel Sheldon at North Castle.

Jameson was not the brightest officer of the Continental army and, having been instructed by Arnold to expect John Anderson to pass through the lines, thought little of the ruckus being made by the three bandits who had delivered this same Anderson into his custody. He looked at the papers taken from André's stocking, recognized the handwriting of Benedict Arnold, examined Arnold's pass for Mr. Anderson, and decided the best thing to do was to forward all the papers, along with Mr. Anderson, to General Arnold's headquarters at Robinson's house.

Shortly after the party left, Major Benjamin Tallmadge, who had been engaged in espionage and intelligence for the Continental army, arrived at Jameson's headquarters, discovered what had happened, and immediately insisted that Jameson bring Mr. Anderson back to his headquarters and send the incriminating papers to General Washington instead of to Arnold. Jameson agreed to recall André, but insisted on sending his letter to Arnold. Finally, in deference to Tallmadge's insistence, Jameson sent the incriminating documents directly to Washington, who was en route from Hartford to West Point.

André, who was being closely guarded by American

troops led by a dragoon who threatened to run him through with his sword should he attempt to escape, was overtaken near Peekskill and returned to North Castle, and then transferred to Lower Salem.

Expecting to be marched to Arnold's headquarters and certain of his immediate release, André continued the guise of John Anderson. However, the next day, Sunday, André discovered that all the documents were being sent directly to Washington, so he asked for a quill and paper and wrote a remarkable letter to the American commander in chief. Dated Salem, September 24, 1780, it read:

I beg your Excellency will be persuaded that no alteration in the temper of my mind, or apprehension for my safety, induces me to take the step of addressing you, but that it is to secure myself from an imputation of having assumed a mean character for treacherous purposes or self-interest, a conduct incompatible with the principles that actuated me, as well as with my condition in life.

It is to vindicate my fame that I speak and not to solicit security.

The person in your possession is Major John André, Adjutant General to the British Army.

The influence of one commander in the army of his adversary is an advantage taken in war. A correspondence for this purpose I held, as confidential (in the present instance) with his Excellency Sir Henry Clinton.

To favor it, I agreed to meet upon ground not within the posts of either Army, a person who was to give me intelligence; I came up in the *Vulture* man-of-war for this effect, and was fetched by a boat from the shore to the beach. Being there, I was told that the approach of day would prevent my return, and that I must be concealed until the next night. I was in my regimentals and had fairly risked my person.

Against my stipulation, my intention, and without my knowledge beforehand, I was conducted within one of your posts. Your Excellency may conceive my sensation on this occasion and will imagine how much more I must have been affected by a refusal to reconduct me back the next night as I had been brought. Thus become a prisoner I had to concert my escape. I quitted my uniform and was passed another way in the night without the American posts to neutral ground, and informed I was beyond all armed parties and left to press for New York. I was taken at Tarry Town by some volunteers.

Thus, as I have had the honor to relate, I was betrayed (being Adjutant General of the British Army) into the vile condition of an enemy in disguise within your posts.

Having avowed myself a British officer, I have nothing to reveal but what relates to myself, which is true on the honor of an officer and a gentleman.

The request I have to make your Excellency, and I am conscious I address myself well, is that in any rigor policy may dictate, a decency of conduct towards me may mark that though unfortunate, I am branded with nothing dishonorable, as no motive could be mine but the service of my kind and as I was involuntarily an impostor."

This letter, along with the papers found on André's person and the passes issued by Arnold, were dispatched hurriedly to Washington at Arnold's headquarters. The rider carrying Jameson's first letter to Arnold apprising him of André's capture, but still ignorant of his true identity, had at least a two-hour lead on the second horseman. The fact that they arrived within less than an hour of one another is an indication of how fast the second rider traveled.

Although the couriers did not arrive until Monday morning, Arnold and Peggy spent an uneasy Sunday, culminating in the return of Smith—who had dined the previous night under the same roof as Washington at Fishkill. Smith told Arnold of his leaving André at the Croton

River, and Arnold realized the dangers André would be exposed to and became even more uneasy.

The nervous tension had heightened by dinnertime, when Arnold's aides, Franks and Varick, and his old friend, John Lamb, sat down to dinner to discover that Smith— whom they all despised heartily—was joining them. Both Franks and Varick had often voiced their dislike of the man, whose brother William was the royal chief justice of New York. Also, they believed that Smith was a secret partner in another of Arnold's get-rich-quick schemes. They suspected that this John Anderson who was given freedom to pass through their lines was probably working closely with Smith and Arnold.

According to Lamb, who had lost an eye fighting with Arnold in Quebec, the dinner proceeded quietly until a servant informed Peggy that they had run out of butter. "Bless me!" Arnold exclaimed, "I had forgot the olive oil I bought in Philadelphia. It will do very well with salt fish."

Arnold informed his guests that the oil had cost him eighty dollars in Continental currency. Smith, always quick with a put-down of the rebel cause, immediately replied that what Arnold meant was that it cost him eighty cents, implying that an American dollar was worth only one cent.

Varick snapped, "That is not true, Mr. Smith."

Lamb added that Varick said this "in such a tone of voice as convinced me you were determined to affront him."

Tempers flared around the table as Smith and Varick shouted at one another, with Franks joining Varick and Arnold taking Smith's position. The bickering continued until Peggy broke in, begging them to drop the argument, as it had raised Arnold's temper to the shouting point.

The meal ended quietly, and Varick, who was not well, went to lie down in the office, where he was later joined by Franks. Both men were bitterly rehashing the argument when Arnold, who had just seen Smith to the door, stormed into the room and began dressing down his aides for their rudeness to his guest.

According to Varick, Arnold "declared that if he asked the devil to dine with him, the gentlemen of his family should be civil to him."

Franks replied that if Smith had not been at Arnold's table, he would have thrown a bottle at him and that he "would thereafter treat him as a rascal."

Varick, sensing physical violence between the two high-tempered men, attempted to divert some of Arnold's rage by taking the blame on himself for having started the argument.

But Franks was not letting anything or anyone stand in the way of what he had to say to Arnold. He told Arnold he was tired of his contant criticism of his conduct, and he requested that he be discharged from Arnold's official family immediately. With that, Franks stormed out of the house and rode to Newburgh. But that didn't shut Arnold up, as Varick testified.

"The dispute between me and Arnold continued very high. I cursed Smith as a damned rascal, a scoundrel, and a spy, and said that my reason for affronting him was that I thought him so."

Varick added that he and Franks advised Arnold against associating with Smith in order to protect Arnold's reputation.

"Arnold then told me that he was always willing to be advised by the gentlemen of his family but, by God, would not be dictated to by them; that he thought he possessed as much prudence as the gentlemen of the family."

That ended the argument, at least for Arnold, who cooled off as quickly as he had exploded. But Varick continued to simmer and later confronted Arnold ". . . and then told him that I considered his past conduct and language to me unwarrantable, and that I thought he did not place that confidence in my repeated friendly assurances and advice which I had a right to expect and which was necessary to put in a person acting in my capacity, and that I could no longer act with propriety."

Despite the vague rhetoric in Varick's speech, the message he was trying to get through to Arnold was that he too was quitting. But Arnold could ill afford to lose such an excellent aide, especially now, so he placated Varick.

"He gave me assurance of his full confidence in me, of a conviction of the rectitude of my conduct, of Smith's being a rascal, and of his error in treating me with such cavalier language; and that he would never go to Smith's house again or be seen with him but in company."

Neither Varick nor Arnold knew at that moment how precisely Arnold would keep this promise, but Arnold was convinced that Smith's services were at an end and he would not need his help once the British seized West Point.

The following morning all hell broke loose in the Arnold household. Arnold was starting breakfast when Colonel Alexander Hamilton arrived with the news that Washington was some fifteen miles to the north and would join the Arnolds for breakfast shortly.

A sudden surge of energy in Washington probably saved Arnold's life. Before reaching the Robinson house, Washington decided he should first inspect some redoubts along the river. He sent two aides ahead to tell the Arnolds to start breakfast without him and his colleagues.

While they were all eating, Colonel Jameson's messenger, Lieutenant Solomon Allen, arrived with a letter for Arnold. Opening it routinely, Arnold read that a man carrying valuable papers about West Point had been captured. He said his name was John Anderson and he was carrying a pass signed by Arnold. Jameson wondered if someone might have forged the General's name. In any case, Jameson continued, the papers had been sent directly to General Washington.

Doing his absolute best to appear unconcerned—one of the greatest theatrical performances in modern history—Benedict Arnold smilingly pocketed the damning letter and rose from the table, excusing himself to attend to Mistress Arnold. No one at the table paid any attention, for such interruptions were routine for a military commander.

Once inside their bedroom, Arnold, his smile now gone, told Peggy quickly what had happened. They both agreed that he must flee to the *Vulture* before Washington reached the Robinson house and discovered Arnold's duplicity. Arnold was worried about Peggy, but she assured him that she could take care of herself. Stuffing two loaded pistols in his belt, Arnold grabbed a few coins and bolted out of the door, nearly knocking over Major Franks, who, having returned from his sulking at Newburgh, brought Arnold news that Washington and his entourage were but minutes away. This news Arnold received with a snort, ordering Franks to have his horse saddled at once and telling him to express his regrets to Washington at not being on hand for his arrival, but important developments required him to barge across the river to West Point. How-

ever, he would be back shortly to greet his Excellency.
Arnold had sent a messenger to the river to alert his barge
oarsmen to stand by for a swift departure and, mounting his
horse, started to gallop toward the river when he met the
first of Washington's party proceeding slowly toward the
Robinson house. Arnold hastily explained that he had urgent business at West Point, but His Excellency should
make himself comfortable and have a pleasant breakfast, by
the end of which Arnold would be back to confer with
him.

Instead of following the regular path to the river,
Arnold spurred his horse down a steep incline, today color-
fully marked by historical signs as "The Traitor's Path."
One who attempts to follow this path ends up in a junk
yard on the shore of the Hudson. Arnold's original route
was direct and led him to his barge, where his boatmen
were sitting around gossiping, snoozing, and rolling dice.
Leaping into the barge, Arnold shouted to his crew to lay
on with gusto in the direction of Stony Point.

The barge was in the middle of the river when a
mounted rider pulled up to the landing and appeared to be
shouting at Arnold. He paid no attention, but urged the
oarsmen on, while the barge sail was raised.

Arnold was terrified that Washington, discovering his
part in the conspiracy, would send express riders to the
forts along the Hudson with orders to fire on his barge—
which is indeed what Washington tried to do the moment
he discovered that Arnold had gone over to the British.
But Arnold had a long enough lead to outdistance any
horseman.

Although he had originally told his bargemen to row
to Stony Point, Arnold now told them to continue on

downriver to the *Vulture*, where he had urgent business to transact. He told them that they must hurry, as he had to be back in time to meet with General Washington. As the barge passed Verplanck's Point opposite Stony Point, Arnold tied a white handkerchief to an oar and put it in the bow. This would hold off any British gunfire and allay any suspicions of American patrol boats.

As the barge pulled alongside the *Vulture*, Arnold shouted for a ladder to be dropped. He climbed onto the deck, shook hands with Colonel Robinson and Captain Sutherland, and briefly told them what he knew about André. Their concern over the Major seemed to overshadow their joy at the arrival in their midst of the great General Arnold, a foreshadowing of things to come.

Arnold's first step, in an attempt to demonstrate his personal charisma, was to announce his change of allegiance to his bargemen, adding that he was now a British general and was raising a brigade of fellow–former rebels. "If you will join me, my lads, I will make sergeants and corporals of you all. And for you, James," he said to the coxswain, Corporal James Larvey, "I will do something more."

The coxswain's reply was immediate.

"No, sir! One coat is enough for me to wear at a time."

His colleagues agreed, and Arnold, infuriated at this humiliation in front of his new British colleagues, demanded that Sutherland take them into custody as prisoners of war.

In his ship's log that night, Sutherland noted: "At ½ pt 11 [11:30 A.M.] Genl Arnold in the American service deliver'd himself up with a boats crew."

At 3:00 P.M. that day, the *Vulture* weighed anchor and set sail down the river to Manhattan and a new life for Benedict Arnold.

PART THREE

14. An Eye for an Eye

WASHINGTON arrived at the Robinson house less than thirty minutes after Arnold galloped down the incline to his barge. Franks told the commander in chief that Arnold had been summoned suddenly to West Point but would be back in an hour. Franks was embarrassed by Arnold's rudeness toward Washington, but Washington was not at all displeased. He had been riding for a couple of hours and his famous appetite was ready for some food.

He told Franks to order breakfast, and said that after eating he and the officers would go to West Point and there confer with Arnold. He left Hamilton at the house and took Knox and Lafayette with him to the fortress, where they spent some time inspecting the defenses, which appeared to be very weak (and which Arnold had complained about in letters to Washington). When he asked Colonel Lamb, who was on duty at the moment, what had become of Arnold, Lamb replied that Arnold had not been to the Point at all that day.

"The impropriety of his conduct when he knew I was to be there struck me very forcibly, and my mind misgave me; but I had not the least idea of the real cause," Washington later recalled.

Once back at the Robinson house, however, Washington rapidly learned the real cause when he opened the packet from Jameson. As Washington read the incriminating documents, he slowly realized that his trusted general had gone over to the British. Shocked though he was, Washington called in Hamilton and Lafayette's aide, Major James McHenry, and told them that Arnold was on his way to join the British and that they should try to stop him. The two men grabbed their pistols and leaped onto their horses. As Lafayette walked into the room Washington was using for an office, the tall Virginian was staring out the window, his shoulders slumped. "My God!" he said, "Arnold has gone over to the British. Whom can we trust now?" He was on the verge of tears, but he composed himself to set a good example for the rest of his staff.

Hamilton returned with a letter for Washington, which Arnold, now safe, had sent from the *Vulture*.

The heart which is conscious of its own rectitude cannot attempt to palliate a step which the world may censure as wrong. I have ever acted from a principle of love to my country since the commencement of the present unhappy contest between Great Britain and the colonies. The same principle of love to my country actuates my present conduct, however it may appear inconsistent to the world, who very seldom judge right of any man's actions.

I have no favor to ask for myself. I have too often experienced the ingratitude of my country to attempt it; but from the known humanity of your Excellency, I am induced to ask your protection for Mrs. Arnold from every insult and injury that the mistaken vengeance of my country may expose her to. It ought to fall only on me; she is as good and as innocent as an angel, and is incapable of doing wrong. I beg she may be permitted to return to her friends in Philadelphia, or to come to me as she may choose; from your Excellency I have no fears on her account, but she may suffer from the mistaken fury of the country.

I have to request that the inclosed letter may be delivered to Mrs. Arnold, and she be permitted to write to me.

I have also to ask that my clothes and baggage, which are of little consequence, may be sent to me; if required their value shall be paid in money.

Arnold generously added this postscript: "In justice to the gentlemen of my family, Colonel Varick and Major Franks, I think myself in honor bound to declare that they, as well as Joshua Smith, Esq. (who I know is suspected), are totally ignorant of any transactions of mine, that they had reason to believe were injurious to the public."

With the exception of the passage about Peggy's innocence, Arnold's letter was completely true. He had no need to exonerate his former attendants, yet he took the time and effort to do so. Varick, Franks, and Smith had no idea what Arnold was planning, and while Smith's character was definitely shady, Varick and Franks worked hard to prove their innocence of any involvement in Arnold's scheme. Varick, who along with Franks was placed under arrest by Washington as soon as he had learned of the conspiracy—both were exonerated—later edited and compiled all the headquarters documents pertaining to the Revolution, became the first mayor of New York City, helped to found the American Bible Society, and finally, in 1824, was buried with great pomp in the churchyard of the First Dutch Reformed Church in Hackensack, New Jersey, where his weather-beaten monument still stands.

Meanwhile, before Washington had received Arnold's letter, he had witnessed a first-rate dramatic performance— Peggy Arnold's pseudo-hysteria following Arnold's departure.

Appearing in a revealing negligee, she screamed at the top of the stairs for Varick, who, sick as he was, climbed up to meet her. She immediately thrashed about hysterically, claiming that Varick was going to assassinate her and her baby. Later, when Washington knew of Arnold's defection, he went to her bedside, where she reviled him and screamed that he and Varick were the commissioned murderers of her child. Washington and Hamilton were much upset by this hysteria, and Arnold's subsequent letter convinced them that Peggy was innocent of any complicity with her husband.

Only later, after Washington had arranged passage for her from West Point to Philadelphia, did she let down her hair and reveal what she really felt. Stopping en route to see Mrs. Theodosia Prevost, widow of a prominent Tory and then engaged to the young Aaron Burr, Peggy confided in Theodosia that she was mightily tired of these histrionics and would be happy once they were over. Theodosia relayed this to Burr, who, to his credit, did not reveal Peggy's duplicity until after she and everyone else involved were dead. Burr, who was no foreigner to the wiles of women, smelled a rat when Peggy's tantrums seemed to explode like clockwork and subside as soon as the appropriate effect had been made. Even before Theodosia told Burr, he suspected Peggy of being phony, but kept his own counsel. For many years, Aaron Burr was reviled by historians for impugning the honor of Peggy Arnold, but publication of the Clinton Papers in 1941 vindicated Burr.

Burr's account, published after his own death, is worthy of consideration: At the Hermitage in Paramus (now in Ho-Ho-Kus):

The frantic scenes of West Point were renewed, and continued so long as strangers were present. Mrs. Prevost was known as the wife of a British officer, and connected with the royalists. In her, therefore, Mrs. Arnold could confide. As soon as they were left alone Mrs. Arnold became tranquillized, and assured Mrs. Prevost that she was heartily sick of the theatrics she was exhibiting. She stated that she had corresponded with the British commander—that she was disgusted with the American cause and those who had the management of public affairs—and that through great persuasion and unceasing perseverance, she had ultimately brought the general into an arrangement to surrender West Point to the British.

It was to Washington's credit that he immediately honored Arnold's request and sent Peggy to Philadelphia, with Major Franks as her escort. The choice of Franks is an interesting one, for he and Varick were officially under suspicion, even though Washington sincerely doubted that they were in the least bit guilty. By assigning Franks to this task, he gave the young officer an opportunity to demonstrate his loyalty and dedication by promptly returning to Washington's camp after delivering Peggy to Philadelphia. Varick and Franks were ultimately cleared completely, but Joshua Smith did not benefit from such swift justice. He was hauled around from camp to camp as a prisoner, ultimately being found innocent by a court-martial.

With Arnold gone, there was the strong likelihood of an attack on West Point, so Washington made every effort to strengthen it. He called upon all available forces, but he was not prepared for the speed with which his request would be answered. Anthony Wayne's unit received the summons at 1:00 A.M., and within the hour they marched, covering sixteen miles in four hours "without a single halt or a man left behind," Wayne recalled proudly.

"When our approach was announced to the General he thought it fabulous, but when convinced of the reality he received us like a god, and retiring to take a short repose exclaimed, 'All is safe, and again I am happy.' "

With the West Point garrison reinforced, Washington turned his attention to Major André. Had André been of lower rank, he most likely would have summarily hanged as a spy. However, the adjutant general of the British army is no ordinary spy, so Washington called for a board of general officers to investigate the case, examine André, and then make recommendations to the commander in chief.

Perhaps no single moment in the American Revolution has been so studied, lamented, and romanticized as the last days of John André. The young staff officer who was widely regarded as a wit and a poet immediately commanded the respect and admiration of his captors. Certainly conscious of the unique position he was in, and probably aware of his ultimate fate, André assumed a dignity that still projects through the nearly two centuries since his death.

Out of a strange concept of correct military etiquette, Washington arranged not to meet André. However, he treated him with respect and consideration.

"I would not wish Mr. André to be treated with insult, but he does not appear on the footing of a common prisoner of war, and therefore he is not entitled to the usual indulgences they receive, and is to be most closely and narrowly watched," Washington wrote to one of the officers in charge of André. The British prisoner was taken first to the Robinson house, then to West Point, where he was lodged in the northeast cell of Fort Putnam, atop the hill overlooking the fort he had schemed with Arnold to capture. On September 28, André was taken by barge to Stony Point, then overland to Tappan, where the court would sit. He was lodged in Casparus Mabie's tavern (which is still in business), just down the dirt road from the Tappan Dutch Reformed Church where the trial would be held.

André's American counterpart, Colonel Alexander Scammell, was determined that André should have no opportunity to escape and, therefore issued a melodramatic order to officers in charge of guarding André.

Major André, the prisoner under your guard, is not only an officer of distinction in the British army, but a man of infinite artfulness and address, who will leave no means unattempted to make his escape and avoid the ignominious death which awaits him. You are therefore, in addition to your sentries [six on the post at all times], to keep two officers constantly in the room with him, with their swords drawn whilst the other officers who are out of the room are constantly to keep walking the entry and round the sentries to see that they are alert.

The guard outside the house consisted of a captain, five subalterns, and forty rank-and-file soldiers.

It is apparent from such an order—it is doubtful that André was so closely watched—that the Americans not only respected André but feared him as well.

On Friday, September 28—a time of year when the trees in the Hudson Valley blaze with gorgeous coloring—André was marched under escort to the church were the board was meeting. The board was headed by General Nathanael Greene, and its members represented the cream of the American army. Included were Major Generals Alexander (who claimed the title Lord Stirling), the Marquis de Lafayette, Baron von Steuben, St. Clair, and Robert Howe. The brigadiers included James Clinton, Glover, Hand, Knox, Parsons, Paterson, and Huntington.

Singularly absent from this impressive roster was General Anthony Wayne, who felt he could not judge André fairly after being the butt of a satiric poem by the young major. Called *The Cow Chace*, the poem mocked Wayne's defeat in a minor skirmish in New Jersey and it held the commander up to ridicule.

André's trial has ever since confounded and confused historians, partly because the participants did not see fit to record minutes. The only first-person account we have is an abstract prepared by the advocate general, the English-born Colonel John Lawrence (who had presented the prosecution's arguments during Benedict Arnold's court-martial).

After Washington's letter ordering the inquiry was read,

The names of the officers composing the board were read to Major André; and on his being asked whether he confessed the matters contained in the letter from his Excellency General Washington to the board, or denied them, he said in addition to his letter to General Washington dated Salem the 24th September, 1780 which was read to the board and acknowledged by Major André to have been written by him . . . that he came on shore from the *Vulture* sloop-of-war in the night of the 21st of September instant, somewhere under the Haverstraw mountain [High Tor]; that the boat he came on shore in carried no flag, and that he had on a surtout coat over his regimentals, and that he wore his surtout coat when he was taken; that he met General Arnold on the shore and had an interview with him there. He also said that when he left the *Vulture* sloop-of-war it was understood he was to return that night, but it was then doubted, and if he could not return he was promised to be concealed on shore in a place of safety

until the next night, when he was to return in the same manner
he came on shore; and when the next day came he was soli-
citous to get back and made inquiries in the course of the day
how he should return, when he was informed he could not
return that way and he must take the route he did afterward.
He also said that the first notice he had of his being within any
of our posts was being challenged by a sentry, which was the
first night he was on shore. He also said that the evening of the
22nd of September instant he passed King's Ferry between our
posts of Stony and Verplanck's Points, in the dress he is at
present in, and which he said is not his regimentals, and which
dress he procured after he landed from the *Vulture* and when
he was within our posts; and that he was proceeding to New
York, but was taken on his way at Tarrytown, as he has mentioned in his letters, on Saturday the 23rd of September instant
about nine o'clock in the morning.

André was shown the papers found on him, as well as
Arnold's pass to John Anderson, and he acknowledged that
he had indeed been carrying them at the time of his capture.

The board having interrogated Major André about his
conception of his coming on shore under the sanction of a
flag, he said that it was impossible for him to suppose he came
on shore under that sanction, and added that if he came on
shore under that sanction he certainly might have returned
under it.

André was asked if he had anything to add, and he
simply said that he left the judgment in the board's hands.

After André was returned to Mabie's Tavern, the
board heard letters from Beverley Robinson, Sir Henry
Clinton, and Benedict Arnold, all insisting that André had
come ashore under a flag and had acted under Arnold's
orders while inside the American lines, and therefore could
not be considered a spy.

But André's own confessions and his refusal to claim

that he had come ashore under such a flag condemned him. It seems now that the board, having heard André's admission of all the evidence, was desperately offering him an honorable excuse to save his neck, but he coolly turned it down.

Why did this materialistic, pleasure-loving, ambitious twenty-nine-year-old officer suddenly throw away his one chance to save his life? No one knows the answer to that question, and there has been endless speculation about it.

One of the more plausible possibilities is that André probably regarded his as a special case, since he was serving as an envoy to Arnold from Sir Henry, following orders much as he would on a battlefield. André felt the court—or else General Washington—should realize that had he been asked to sneak into the American lines as a common spy for pay, he would have turned down that request indignantly. Even though his outward behavior was that of a spy, André hoped that his position as a gentleman and a high-ranking staff officer of the British army would encourage his judges to consider his intentions rather than the external circumstances which had led to his capture.

But the board was pragmatic, and knew that André would be judged by all Americans as a spy. Also, it was well known throughout the American camp that Washington was determined to set a horrible example to deter other would-be Benedict Arnolds.

Therefore, the board concluded "that Major André, adjutant general to the British army, ought to be considered as a spy from the enemy; and that, agreeable to the law and usage of nations, it is their opinion that he ought to suffer death."

In the general orders the next day, Washington approved the sentence and ordered the execution to take place at 5:00 P.M. the following day, October 1.

André received his sentence calmly and asked that he be granted permission to write to General Clinton, which was granted. Meanwhile, Clinton, Robinson, and Arnold had been bombarding Washington with letters that contained pleas, rational appeals, threats, and extravagant offers of exchange. Clinton wanted desperately to save his brilliant young adjutant, and he informed Washington that he had several American officers in custody who had been taken in far more compromising circumstances than André, yet he had spared their lives. Arnold wrote to Washington in a belligerent tone that if André was executed, he would personally prevail upon Clinton to seek revenge in the execution of all American prisoners in British hands.

But Washington was adamant. When he received word from Sir Henry that he had some persuasive arguments to present, Washington obligingly postponed the execution for one day, scheduling it for October 2 at noon. But Clinton's arguments, presented by General James Robertson to Washington's representative, General Nathanael Greene, consisted of the same ones which the board had already requested.

Not all the American officers were happy with the board's sentence, and several talked about posible ways to free André. The most intensive effort on André's behalf was carried out by Washington's aide, Alexander Hamilton. Apparently the stern-visaged commander in chief would be willing to exchange André to the British in return for one man—Benedict Arnold.

Hamilton hurriedly wrote a note to Sir Henry Clinton,

which he had sent to British headquarters as rapidly as possible. He didn't sign it, but everyone who knew Hamilton at that time testified that it was in his handwriting, and even Clinton noted Hamilton's authorship and assumed he was speaking unofficially for Washington.

Referring to André, Hamilton wrote:

> Though an enemy his virtues and his accomplishments are admired. Perhaps he might be released for General Arnold, delivered up without restriction or condition, which is the prevailing wish. Major André's character and situation seem to demand this of your justice and friendship. Arnold appears to have been the guilty author of the mischief and ought more properly to be the victim, as there is great reason to believe he meditated a double treachery and had arranged the interview in such a manner that if discovered in the first instance, he might have it in his power to sacrifice Major André to his own safety.

Hamilton added a postscript: "No time is to be lost."

Other American officers suggested that this appeal might carry more weight if André himself made the appeal, for Clinton could not turn down his beloved aide. But Hamilton refused to make such a suggestion to André, knowing what the major's answer would be. "As a man of honor he could but reject it, and I would not for the world have proposed to him a thing which must have placed me in the unamiable light of supposing him capable of meanness, or of not feeling myself the impropriety of the measure."

Although by Clinton's notation at the bottom of Hamilton's letter, it was not received until after André's death, the question of exchanging Arnold for André was unthinkable. After all, it was Clinton's clear duty to encourage as many rebels as possible to renounce the patriot cause and return to the King's service. Also, Clinton had promised Arnold protection and reward, and he was speaking with the King's authority. To hand Arnold over to the Americans for certain hanging would have been to betray his word as well as the King's, and such a move would certainly discourage any future defectors.

When André realized that his death was imminent, he wrote to Washington asking that at least he be shot like a soldier rather than hang as a spy.

> Sympathy towards a soldier will surely induce your Excellency and a military tribunal to adopt the mode of my death to the feelings of a man of honor.
>
> Let me hope, Sir, that if aught in my character impresses you with esteem towards me, if aught in my misfortunes marks me as the victim of policy and not of resentment, I shall experience the operation of these feelings in your breast, by being informed that I am not to die on a gibbet.

Washington was placed in the difficult position of wanting to grant André's request but being incapable of doing it. André had been convicted as a spy, and the penalty for spying was hanging. To have shot André would have been to raise the entire question of his guilt, and Washington knew what a hornet's nest such a controversy could stir up.

In recalling his frequent visits to André, Alexander Hamilton observed:

> When his sentence was announced to him he remarked that since it was his lot to die, there was still a choice in the mode, which would make a material difference in his feelings, and he would be happy, if possible, to be indulged with a professional death. . . . It was thought this indulgence, being incompatible with the customs of war, could not be granted, and it was therefore determined . . . to evade an answer to

spare him the sensations which a certain knowledge of the intended mode would inflict.

In one of his earlier visits, Hamilton was asked by André to see that his farewell letter to Clinton was delivered.

I foresee my fate [he told Hamilton], and though I pretend not to play the hero, to be indifferent about life, yet I am reconciled to whatever may happen, conscious that misfortune, not guilt, has brought it upon me. There is only one thing that disturbs my tranquility. Sir Henry Clinton has been too good to me; he has been lavish of his kindness. I am bound to him by too many obligations and love him too well to bear the thought that he should reproach himself, or that others should reproach him, on the supposition of my having conceived myself obliged by his instructions to run the risk I did. I would not for the world leave a sting that in his mind should imbitter his future days.

At this point, André broke down. According to Hamilton, "He could scarce finish the sentence, bursting into tears in spite of his efforts to suppress them, and with difficulty collected himself afterwards . . ."

A few hours before his execution, André, seated in front of a mirror, made a pen-and-ink sketch of himself, which he left with Ensign Jabez Tomlinson, an officer of the guard. His breakfast was sent over, as it had been since his captivity, from the table of General Washington, and he then summoned a barber to shave him and do his hair. His servant had been allowed through the lines to bring a dress uniform, and it was with relief and pride that he finally donned the regimentals of a British staff officer. He packed his trunk and gave his keys to his servant, who, according to some accounts, was blubbering so loudly that André sent him from the room until he could compose himself. One thing was certain: André was going to give these rebels a stunning example of how a British officer goes to his death.

Linking his arms with Ensign Samuel Bowman and Captain John Hughes, André said, "I am ready at any time, gentlemen, to wait on you." Then he led them through the doors of Mabie's Tavern and into the bright noonday light of a glorious autumn day. The entire American army was drawn up along the route André marched to his execution, and the path was also crowded with civilians who had heard about the handsome young major who was to die for Benedict Arnold.

Smiling and chatting with his escorts, André complimented the musicians on their excellent playing. Along the route were the members of the court who had doomed André. Each he saluted with a bow of the hat, and each returned the salute.

As the execution party climbed the hill west of Tappan, André got his first look at the gallows awaiting him. The accounts of his reaction vary widely, as do the words he is supposed to had said. Some of those witnesses who later reported his conversation actually were standing several yards away. The only man near André at that awful moment, and who later noted his words, was Ensign Bowman.

"I have borne myself with fortitude but this is too degrading!" André exclaimed, according to Bowman. "As respects myself, it is a matter of no consequence, but I have a mother and a sister who will be much mortified by the intelligence."

Perhaps André did not speak so stiffly, but all the observers agree that he was chagrined that his request to be shot like a soldier had been turned down. And the man who had turned down that request sat glumly in the De Windt House, ordering his aides to draw the shutters so he would not have to hear the noises surrounding the execution of such a brave young soldier.

The horse-drawn cart containing André's coffin—painted black—was drawn up beneath the unusually high beams of the gallows. With some effort, André climbed onto the cart and then onto the top of the coffin and, as most observers agree, paced back and forth the length of the box, with his arms akimbo.

As spectators and soldiers in the crowd sobbed softly, André removed his hat and neckpiece. When the hangman, with his face and hands smeared with tar to prevent recognition, approached, André repulsed him and took the noose and settled it around his neck, tightening it beneath his right ear. Then he pulled forth a handkerchief and covered his eyes with it.

The American adjutant general, Colonel Scammell, who was in charge of the execution, pointed out that André's arms must be pinioned. André removed his blindfold and took another scarf from his pocket and handed it to the hangman, who tied his arms gently above the elbows after André had returned the blindfold to his eyes.

The hangman then scampered up one of the uprights of the gallows to attach the end of the rope, as Colonel Scammell, his voice quavering slightly, said:

"Major André, you have but a few moments left to live. Do you have anything to say?"

André's voice was not loud, but in the hush it seemed to carry for miles.

"Only that you all bear witness that I die like a soldier

and a brave man."

Scammell raised his sword, the muffled drums rolled, and the hangman cracked a whip across the horses' rumps. The cart jumped out from beneath André, the drop killing him instantly.

Now that the Americans had exacted their eye for an eye, they could afford to be generous in their praise of the human sacrifice. Washington had kind words, as did Hamilton, Tallmadge, and many others who knew André during his final days. These oratorical and literary garlands have been repeated so often in other works that it is not necessary to rehash them. Suffice it to say that Americans felt guilty at taking the life of the gallant young Major John André.

Back in New York, Clinton had been anxiously awaiting reply to his most recent pleas to Washington when André's servant arrived, carrying his clothes and belongings and the terrible tale of his execution. Clinton, who had feared the worst from the start but had continued to hope that Washington would listen to reason, was stunned. On October 8, he issued the following orders:

> The Commander in chief does with infinite regret inform the army of death of the adjutant general, Major André.
>
> The unfortunate fate of this officer calls upon the commander in chief to declare his opinion that he ever considered Major André as a gentleman as well as in the line of his military profession of the highest integrity and honor, and incapable of any base action or unworthy conduct.
>
> Major André's death is very severely felt by the commander in chief, as it assuredly will be by the army, and must prove a real loss to His Majesty's service.

The evening of the same day that Clinton issued this statement, he received a peremptory note from Washington informing him that a number of citizens of Charleston, South Carolina, following the capture of that town by the British, had been thrown into a prison ship. Washington concluded his note with these words: "You will oblige me by making the communication as soon as convenient."

Sir Henry could hardly believe such a cold-blooded letter from the killer of his dearest friend. Not wasting a minute, Clinton dictated the following letter, which under the circumstances was a masterpiece of irony.

Persuaded it is for the interest of mankind that a correspondence should exist between generals commanding adverse armies, I do, without waiting your return to applications of an earlier date made on my part on a subject very interesting to me, answer without delay your letter . . .

I have heard the report you mention, that a number of persons under the capitulation of Charleston, had entered into a plot for the destruction of the place where they are protected, and that the officer commanding there had found it necessary to interfere. I have this only from common fame [rumor]; no report has been made to me on the subject.

But as I am well acquainted with Lord Cornwallis's humanity, I cannot entertain the least apprehension that he will stain the lustre of the King's arms by acts of cruelty. The friends of those persons under the description you give of them need be under no fears for their safety. Lord Cornwallis is incapable of straining the laws to take away the lives or liberties of the innocent. If any forced construction be put upon the laws by his Lordship, it will be in favor of the accused, and every plea their friends can offer for them will be humanely heard and respected.

> I am Sir,
> Your most h[ble] Servant
> H. CLINTON

Whether Washington read into this letter all the bitterness and sorrow racking Sir Henry is unknown. Washington had ordered the death of André, so he was forced to defend his action. Even the officers of the court, who were said to have signed the sentence with tear-filled eyes, never backed down from the assumption that what they did was the price of warfare.

Clinton's letter, which has rarely been quoted, illustrates not only his bitterness but also some of the feeling of the entire British army for the popular young major. And who did the British get in trade for André? Benedict Arnold.

Even though Arnold did his best to write letters on André's behalf, and even if he did make the offer to surrender himself to the Americans in order to free André—an offer which he could have made, knowing that Clinton would never accept it—Arnold had failed in his effort to become a second General Monk.

Instead of being regarded as a hero, he was dismissed as a traitor who had cost the British army a valuable officer. Also, he had failed completely in the scheme to surrender West Point, so what good was he to the British?

15. The Fallen Eagle

ARNOLD had originally foreseen a triumphant reception in New York, but now the only politeness he received was from Sir Henry—who had to strain himself to smile and patronize the man responsible for the death of his adjutant general—and Judge William Smith, Joshua's brother. Senior officers were deferential to Arnold, but the junior officers—Andre's friends—hated him with an open passion and took every opportunity to snub him. One of Arnold's new functions was to raise a military unit among loyalists and defecting patriots, and he could not find any young British officers to assist him.

Also, Arnold became aware of plots to smuggle patriots into New York in the guise of defectors to capture him by night and bring him across the river for summary execution. Many months later, when Arnold was leading an expedition to Virginia and encountered a captured American officer, he inquired what his fate would be should the Americans capture him. The rebel officer replied immediately that Arnold's left leg, which had been wounded at Quebec and Saratoga, would be cut off and given a formal military burial, then the rest of the traitor would be hanged from the nearest gallows.

Such sentiments did not fill Arnold with compassion toward his former colleagues. With Clinton's blessing, Ar-

nold mounted an expedition to raid and destroy the priva-
teering ports of New London and Groton, Connecticut,
not far from where he grew up.

The raids were successful, but two things went wrong
that further tarred Arnold's name in the rebel colonies. The
first was a strong easterly wind that blew the flames from
the blazing ammunition depots in New London through
the entire town, reducing it to ashes. The other incident
was observed by Arnold in horror from the opposite side
of the river. His troops stormed Fort Griswold, and were
repulsed with many losses. Finally they captured the fort
and, in a bloody blind rage, set about butchering all the
occupants who had thrown down their arms and called for
quarter. Arnold had never indulged in such vicious blood-
letting, and he was horrified at the sight of American
corpses strewn about the fort. Many of his former child-
hood friends placed all the blame on Arnold's head, not
only for the slaughter but for the burning of New London.
In addition, he had lost too many of his own troops for
Clinton ever again to trust him with command of a large
expedition.

Meanwhile, Arnold had been paid £6,000 for his defection by the British, substantially less than the £10,000
Arnold had demanded and claimed that André had agreed
to during their meeting. He was also issued a permanent
commission as a cavalry colonel, with a temporary commission as brigadier general, with pay of £450 per year
until the end of the war, then half that amount yearly for
the rest of his life. As a provincial brigadier, Arnold received an additional £200 yearly until the war was over.

One of the most interesting awards, after the war
ended in 1783, however, was a grant by the King to Peggy

—who had joined Benedict with their children in New York—of an annual pension of £500 for the rest of her life, plus a pension for each of Peggy's and Arnold's five surviving children. Arnold's three sons by his first marriage all received commissions in the British army, with appropriate salaries deliverable to their parent until they were old enough to serve.

Following the surrender of Cornwallis at Yorktown in October of 1781 (when Alexander Scammell, the presiding officer at Andre's execution, was fatally shot in the back by British soldiers—after he had surrendered—almost one year to the day after André's death), Arnold concluded that his future would be brighter in England. On December 15, 1781, Arnold and Peggy and the children sailed on separate ships for England and a new life.

In London, the Arnolds were met with mixed reactions. The Tories, who were on the verge of being toppled from power, treated them affably, and King George personally summoned Arnold for several audiences. The Prince of Wales—heir apparent to the throne and the future George IV—made a point of strolling arm in arm with the hawk-nosed American hero in the public gardens of London. The Queen took Peggy under her wing and favored her openly.

However, the pro-war Tory party had lost public confidence by waging a senseless, costly war in a distant land, and the government's opponents, the Whigs, were contemptuous toward the general they regarded as a traitor.

Aside from exiled American Tories, Arnold found friendship with some of his former foes. One of his closest friends turned out to be Sir Guy Carleton, the man with whom Arnold had dueled in such an uneven contest during

the snowstorm at Quebec. Another friend was Lord Cornwallis, and another was Sir Henry Clinton. Cornwallis and
Clinton both regarded Arnold as a symbol for what they
had been trying to achieve in the rebel colonies—a rational
return to British rule. But Sir Guy Carleton, who was perhaps the only British general who could match Arnold
move for move in strategy and cunning, took the embattled defector and introduced him to all the right Tory
families.

On one occasion, Sir Guy suggested that the two of
them attend a meeting of Parliament, to test the sentiment
of British lawmakers toward the man who had risked his
neck to bring an end to the American war. But the members of the House of Commons were not nearly as cordial
as Arnold had expected. One excited member asked that
the infamous traitor be summarily thrown out of the sacred
chambers, but Arnold haughtily stalked out before any action could be taken on the request.

After several futile attempts to start new business ventures in London, and financially crippled by Peggy's taste
for the luxuries of life, Arnold decided to move to St.
John, in New Brunswick, to set up a shipping and trading
company.

Arnold prospered long enough in the Canadian prov-
ince to summon Peggy to join him. Then a series of financial disasters hit him and, when he found that many of the
American exiles in St. John regarded him as a scoundrel,
Arnold sold his property and returned to England.

Events in Europe were marching, and by 1789 the
French Revolution was in full flower. After the French
guillotined King Louis XVI, the patron of the American
Revolution, the British declared war on France. Arnold

immediately offered his services in the forthcoming war, but was viciously snubbed.

Arnold started more trading companies, while Peggy continued to conceive children, losing most of them before or just after birth. One memorable event of these lean years stands out. Arnold traveled from London to Falmouth to await a ship of his which was due that day in 1794. He stopped in at a waterfront tavern for some food, and he suddenly found himself the subject of attention from a Frenchman who was fleeing the Reign of Terror in France for a brief exile in America, and whose ship had been so battered by a storm that it had to lay in at Falmouth for repairs. The Frenchman reports the following incident:

> The innkeeper at whose place I had my meals informed me that one of his lodgers was an American general. Thereupon I expressed the desire of seeing that gentleman and, shortly after, I was introduced to him. After the usual exchange of greetings, I put to him several questions concerning his country but, from the first, it seemed to me that my inquiries annoyed him. Having several times vainly endeavored to renew the conversation, which he always allowed to drop, I ventured to request from him some letters of introduction to his friends in America.
>
> "No," he replied, and after a few moments of silence, noticing my surprise, he added, "I am perhaps the only American who cannot give you letters for his own country . . . all the relations I had there are now broken . . . I must never return to the States."
>
> He dared not tell me his name. It was General Arnold. I must confess that I felt much pity for him, for which political puritans will perhaps blame me, but with which I do not reproach myself, for I witnessed his agony.

The mysterious visitor with Arnold was an obscure former bishop from Périgord and the future confidant and overthrower of Napoleon, Charles Maurice de Talleyrand.

This is a meeting to give playwrights and novelists—not to mention historians—goose bumps! Talleyrand was at various points in his long and devious life the friend of Arnold's former field colleagues, Lafayette and the Duc de Lauzun, later intimate with Robespierre and Danton, John Paul Jones and Thomas Paine. And he would ultimately serve and destroy a military genius comparable to Benedict Arnold, Napoleon Bonaparte.

The brief meeting of Talleyrand and Arnold might be compared to that of Beethoven and Mozart, Benjamin Franklin and Voltaire.

Shortly after his meeting with Talleyrand, Arnold found himself in the West Indies, where he carried on a brisk trade. But he was caught in the warfare between England and France and, when the French fleet hemmed him in at St. Kitts, he declared that he was an American merchant named John Anderson!

But the French were suspicious of him and took him prisoner. Arnold had concealed money on his person, and once the English fleet was sighted on the horizon, he bribed the crew of the ship to provide him with a cask in which to hide his personal belongings and a raft with which he could make his escape to the British. Darting among the French ships, he made it to the English flagship and eventually even recovered the cask containing his personal belongings.

For a few months, Arnold engaged in the war in the West Indies as an unofficial aide to Sir Charles Grey, André's former patron. Arnold never achieved the intimacy with Grey that André had won, and after several months he returned to England.

By 1795, when he returned, Peggy was virtually an invalid, slowly being eaten away by cancer. The years dragged on, and Arnold spent them caring for his wife and his family, and also trying to stave off creditors. Each new windfall was gobbled up by the vultures who were once again preying on Benedict Arnold. By 1800, he was racked with asthma, gout in his right leg, and recurrent pains in his wounded leg. His military future was nil, and his past only seemed to bring him opprobrium.

During the Arnolds' stay in England, they visited Westminster Abbey, and we have an account of one such visit from H. C. van Schaack, writing about his Tory relative Peter van Schaack, who was then living in London.

In one of Mr. van Schaack's visits to the Abbey, some time after Arnold's treason, his musings were interrupted by the entrance of a gentleman accompanied by a lady. It was General Arnold and the lady was doubtless Mrs. Arnold. They passed to the cenotaph of Major André, where they stood and conversed together. What a spectacle! The traitor Arnold in Westminster Abbey, at the tomb of André, deliberately perusing the monumental inscription, which will transmit to future ages his own infamy.

The monument studied by the Arnolds was not André's tomb, for his bones were not returned from America and interred beneath the monument until long after Arnold and Peggy were dead. However, shortly after André's death, a memorial was erected to his memory in Westminster Abbey, and this is doubtless what van Schaack saw.

As for Arnold and Peggy's visiting the cenotaph, why not? Arnold himself was not guilty of André's death—he had done everything possible to prevent it. And the two had conversed cordially for a few hours. Also, Peggy was a close friend of André's.

By early 1801, Benedict Arnold's health was rapidly

declining, with his asthma worsening and his gout becoming excruciating. He was surrounded by people who did not understand him. Englishmen, who should have honored him for his noble sacrifice, sneered at him as a traitor, while Tories regarded him as a pathetic failure.

The end of Benedict Arnold's long suffering came on June 14, 1801.

Peggy described his last years with compassion, telling how "the numerous vexations and mortifications he has endured had so broken his spirit and destroyed his nerves that he has been for a long time past incapable of the smallest enjoyment . . ."

His legs had swollen, the left throbbing still with the wounds from Quebec and Saratoga, the right with gout, and both with dropsy. His breathing became increasingly more difficult and painful.

"Every alarming and distressing symptom rapidly increased and, after great suffering, he expired Sunday morning, the 14th of June at ½ past six in the morning, without a groan," Peggy wrote.

The newspapers took only passing notice of his death. One account says that seven mourning coaches and four state carriages formed the funeral procession, one of which carried Lord Cornwallis.

Benedict Arnold was buried in the crypt of St. Mary's in Battersea, and was joined three years later by Peggy—who by then had completely liquidated all of Arnold's debts and had enabled her sons to move on in their careers without the stigma of poverty.

16. The Romantic Legend of John André

EVEN BEFORE he was dead, Major André aroused the sympathy and excited the romantic imagination of both British and Americans. His walk to the gallows was witnessed by many sobbing women and girls, and there were several American officers whose lips were quivering at the sight of the handsome young major going so cheerfully to his death.

When his body was cut down from the gallows and laid in the black wooden coffin, local women covered him with garlands and flowers. Local residents immediately marked his grave with stones and rocks and planted two cedar trees alongside it. A peach tree sprang up from the head of the grave, possibly taking root from the peach handed to André on his way to the gallows by a young Tappan girl. Another legend is that this same girl planted a peach tree over André's shallow grave. However it took root, a peach tree and two cedars did indeed mark the grave of André for forty years.

News of André's tragic death spread rapidly throughout England, and he became a romantic hero. Miss Seward, with whom he had spent so much time, composed a song,

"Monody on the Death of Major André," which was widely printed.

Shortly after the war, a movement began to erect a monument to André in Westminster Abbey, the burial place of England's great. The monument was inscribed:

Sacred to the memory of Major John André who, raised by his merit at an early period of life to the rank of Adjutant-General of the British forces in America and, employed in an important but hazardous enterprise, fell a sacrifice to his zeal for his King and Country, on the 2nd of October, 1780, aged 29, universally beloved and esteemed by the army in which he served, and lamented even by his foes. His gracious Sovereign, King George III, has caused this monument to be erected.

A monument was one thing, but the fact that the body of the man the monument commemorated lay buried beneath the site of his gallows in distant America continued to trouble the British.

It was not until after peace had been made following the War of 1812 (during which the British had stormed the young nation's capital city of Washington and burned both the Capitol and the White House), that talk of removing André's bones to Westminster once again started. Acting on behalf of the Duke of York, the British consul in New York, James Buchanan, made arrangements to transfer the hero's remains in 1821. His account is fascinating.

Upon reaching the village of Tappan, "which does not contain above fifty or sixty houses, the first we inquired at proved to be the very house in which the Major had been confined while a prisoner there." The proprietor of Mabie's Tavern "took us to view the room which had been used as a prison."

Excited as we were [the account goes on], it would be difficult to describe our feelings on entering this little chamber; it was then used as a milk and store-room—otherwise unaltered from the period of his confinement—about twelve feet by eight, with one window looking into the garden, the view extending to the hill and directly to the spot on which he suffered—as the landlord pointed out from the window while in the room, the trees growing at the place where he was buried.

Having inquired for the owner of the field, I waited on the Rev. Mr. Demarest, a Minister residing in Tappan, to whom I explained the object of my visit, and who generously expressed his satisfaction at the honor "which at length," to use his words, "was intended the memory of Major André," and assured me that every facility should be afforded by him. Whereupon we all proceeded to examine the grave attended by many of the inhabitants, who by this time had become acquainted with the cause of our visit; and it was truly gratifying to us, as it was honorable to them, that all were loud in the expressions of their gratification on this occasion.

We proceeded up a narrow lane, or broken road, with trees on each side which obscured the place where he suffered, until we came to the opening into the field which at once led to an elevated spot on the hill. On reaching the mount, we found it commanded a view of the surrounding countryside for miles. General Washington's headquarters and the house in which he resided [the DeWindt House] was distant about a mile and a half or two miles, but fully in view. The army lay encamped chiefly in view of the place and must necessarily have witnessed the catastrophe.

The field, as well as I could judge, contained from eight to ten acres and was cultivated; but around the grave the plow had not approached nearer than three or four yards—that space being covered with loose stone thrown upon and around the grave, which was only indicated by two cedar trees about ten feet high; a small peach tree had also been placed at the head of the grave by the kindly feeling of a lady in the neighborhood.

Many expressed the belief that the body had been secretly

carried to England, but these surmises were set aside by the more general testimony of the community. . . .

Buchanan apparently returned to New York, showing up again in Tappan on August 10, 1821, "though I had not been expected until the following Tuesday, as I had fixed, yet a number of persons soon assembled, some of whom betrayed symptoms of displeasure at the proceeding, arising from the observations of some of the public journals which asserted 'That any honor paid Major André was casting imputation on General Washington, and the officers who tried André.' "

Though these characters were of the lowest cast [he continued], and their observations were condemned by every respectable person in the village, I yet deemed it prudent, while the worthy pastor was preparing his men to open the grave, to resort to a mode of argument—the only one I had time or inclination to bestow on them—in which I was sure to find the landlord a powerful auxiliary. I therefore stated to these noisy patriots that I wished to follow a custom not infrequent in Ireland, from whence I came, namely, of taking some spirits before proceeding to a grave. The landlord approved the Irish practice and accordingly supplied abundance of liquor, so that in a short time General Washington, Major André, and the object of my visit were forgotten by them, and I was left at perfect liberty with the respectable inhabitants of the place to proceed to the exhumation, leaving the landlord to supply the guests—a duty which he faithfully performed to my entire satisfaction.

At twelve o'clock quite an unexpected crowd assembled at the grave—as our proceeding up the hill was seen by the inhabitants all around.

The day was unusually fine; a number of ladies and many aged matrons who witnessed his fall—who had mingled tears with his sufferings—attended, and were loud in their praise of the prince for thus at length honoring one who still lived in their recollection with unsubdued sympathy. The labors proceeded with dilligence, yet caution; surmises about the body having been removed were revived, and it would be difficult to imagine any event which could convey a degree of more excitement.

As soon as the stones were cleared away and the grave was found, not a tongue moved amongst the multitude—breathless anxiety was depicted in every countenance.

When at length one of the men cried out that he had touched the coffin, so great was the enthusiasm at this moment that I found it necessary to call the aid of several of the ladies to form an enlarged circle, so that all could see the operation; which being effected, the men proceeded with the greatest caution and the clay was removed with the hands, as we soon discovered the lid of the coffin was broken in the center.

With great care the broken lid was removed, and there to our view lay the bones of the brave André, in perfect order. I, amongst others, for the first time discovered that he had been a small man.

This observation I made from the skeleton, which was confirmed by some then present. The roots of the small peach tree had completely surrounded the skull like a net.

"After allowing all the people to pass around in regular order and view the remains as they lay, which very many did with unfeigned tears and lamentations, the bones were carefully removed and placed in the sarcophagus (the circle having again been formed), after which I descended into the coffin, which was not more than three feet below the surface, and with my own hands raked the dust together to ascertain whether he had been buried in his regimentals or not, as it was rumored by the assemblage that he was stripped; for if buried in his regimentals, I expected to find the buttons of his clothes which would have disproved the rumor. But I did not find a single button, nor any article save a string of leather that had bound his hair at the time. This string I forwarded to his sister in England.

What Buchanan did not know, but which had been revealed by an eyewitness to the execution, an artificer in Colonel Jeduthun Baldwin's regiment, was that shortly before André's body was laid in its coffin, his servants from New York removed his regimentals to take back with them. But rumors and distortions had raised the suspicion that the Americans had deliberately stripped André's body as a final degradation.

Buchanan had the sarcophagus removed to the Reverend Demarest's house, then transferred to a British ship in New York. While it lay in Demarest's parlor, the sarcophagus was continually covered by flowers from the local women.

On November 28, 1821, André's remains reached their final resting place in Westminster Abbey. In his *Historical Memorials of Westminster Abbey*, Arthur Penrhyn Stanley, Dean of Westminster, describes some of the many graves in the Abbey.

> The unfortunate General Burgoyne, whose surrender at Saratoga lost America to England lies, without a name, in the North Cloister. But of that great struggle, the most conspicuous trace is left on the southern wall of the Nave by the memorial of the ill-fated Major André, whose remains, brought home after a lapse of forty years, lie close beneath."

A private service was held in the Abbey, with Sir Herbert Taylor representing the Duke of York and another gentleman representing the surviving sisters of the young hero.

Arthur Penrhyn Stanley was no ordinary Dean of Westminster. During his tenure during the final decades of the nineteenth century, the Abbey was ripped up, rebuilt, and sagging floors fortified. During that time he had the incredible experience of peering into royal graves, discovering which king was buried with which queen, the details of which fill his fascinating two-volume study.

However, Dean Stanley had a warm feeling for Major André, and during 1879—ninety-nine years after the death of André—while he was visiting Cyrus W. Field in Irvington, New York, Stanley suggested that Field erect a monument to André on the site of his execution and burial. This was done three times, the first two monuments having been dynamited by anti-British fanatics or discontented Irishmen.

Today, however, the monument stands peacefully, surrounded by an iron grille fence with a gate which is never locked. One can no longer see the DeWindt House because of the cluster of houses and trees surrounding the monument. The inscription, clearly visible, reads:

Here died October 2, 1780 Major John André of the British Army who, entering the American lines on a secret mission to Benedict Arnold for the surrender of West Point, was taken prisoner, tried, and condemned as a spy. His death, though according to the stern code of war, moved even his enemies to pity, and both armies mourned the fate of one so young and so brave. In 1821 his remains were removed to Westminster Abbey. A hundred years after his execution this stone was placed above the spot where he lay by a citizen of the states against which he fought, not to perpetuate the record of strife, but in token of the better feelings which have since united two nations, one in race, in language, and in religion, with the earnest hope that this friendly union will never be broken.

—ARTHUR PENRHYN STANLEY, DEAN OF WESTMINSTER

On the opposite side of the monument is another inscription:

He was more unfortunate than criminal
An accomplished man and a gallant officer
—GEORGE WASHINGTON

Epilogue

BENEDICT ARNOLD has not had a fair shake from historians, particularly those Americans who find it easy to vilify Arnold while rhapsodizing over the romantic, tragic Major André. The simplistic view propounded is that in spite of his monumental achievements for the young nation, Benedict Arnold can never be forgiven his decision to change sides.

Perhaps America today is entering an era of realistic appraisal of its own history, an era when concepts of patriotism and treason lose some of their black-and-white, right-or-wrong connotations. One reason to hope for this national maturity is the growing public sympathy toward the young men who have fled their country in order to avoid taking part in a war they regarded as immoral. To them, America's position in Indochina is not unlike Britain's position in the colonies during the Revolution. This particular parallel can be carried only so far, but it is mentioned to show how national tolerances change. During World War II, any man who shirked military duty was considered a coward and any man who would flee to a neutral nation to avoid conscription was a traitor. Even within our own second half of the twentieth century, we have seen the execution of human beings as spies and traitors.

Perhaps Americans are ready to accept a dispassionate examination of Benedict Arnold, what he was and why he decided to change sides. There is no question that he was a great general, and there also is no question that he was treated shabbily by Congress in the business of his promotion. And he certainly was harassed by the Pennsylvania council. On the other side of the issue, Arnold frequently engaged in business dealings that bordered on being unethical or involved a conflict of interest. He had a sensitive ego and an inflated concept of his personal honor, and he was filled with self-righteousness.

But does any of this add up to the monster Benedict Arnold has been painted to be? Would a wounded ego or a congressional rebuff be enough to push Arnold into the arms of the British? Some historians think that Washington's reprimand was the final sting, but despite his highly emotional letters, Arnold must have known that Washington bore him no ill will personally and was only following his orders. And at the earliest opportunity, Washington offered Arnold a position of honor in the Continental army.

All the evidence from the Clinton Papers indicates that Arnold had made up his mind *before* his court-martial. Bitterness certainly was a factor in Arnold's decision, as was the prospect of receiving a large sum of money—something his Americans had refused him, even after he had spent his own gold on their behalf.

We are left with one conclusion, and that is to take Arnold's own explanation at face value: That he defected to the British in order to hasten the end of the war, a war which he was convinced the Americans could never win.

This argument can be (and has been) attacked as hypocrisy and self-vindication. But then, we really have no other tenable argument to explain Arnold's behavior. Perhaps he really was convinced that the war was lost, that Congress was inept, that the Continental army was composed of inferior soldiers and led by inferior officers, without plans, strategy, or tactics.

To such reasoning the traditional historian replies that with Washington at the head of the army, the American cause was invincible. Well, Benedict Arnold had a closer view of Washington than any historian, and while he admired the man deeply, what he saw may have disturbed him. An army and a nation which depends on the charisma of one man had better have a strong man in that role, and Arnold could see at close range how vulnerable Washington was. The commander in chief had been worn down by years of defeat to the point of fatigue. Arnold, who had often ordered Dan Morgan's riflemen to pick off British officers during battle, perhaps was aware how vulnerable a target Washington was, sitting tall atop his white mare. One British musket bullet could have wiped out the entire American cause, if that cause hung solely on Washington's presence.

Once Arnold made up his mind to change sides, his first suggestion was that the British surprise and capture Washington while he was crossing the Hudson with only a small guard. Arnold recognized Washington's greatness, yet he also understood how frail the American cause really was and how the capture or killing of the one supreme leader could wipe out the rebellion in just days, possibly weeks.

Another argument Arnold advanced publicly for his changing sides was the French alliance. Arnold said he was afraid that a French victory would impose French (and Catholic) rule on Protestant America. This particular argument may have been made just to impress the British, for Arnold had not expressed anti-French feelings before he decided to join the British.

The more one studies the enigma of Benedict Arnold, the more it is possible to accept Arnold's explanation as it stands. Throughout his early correspondence with the British are references to General Monk, who changed sides at just the right moment in history and became a hero. Unless Arnold felt that the American cause was doomed, it seems unlikely that he would have defected when he did, at a time when he knew that Washington was considering him for a major position.

And accepting Arnold's explanation as an honest declaration enables us to sweep aside some of the enigmatic cobwebs which have obscured posterity's vision of this remarkable man for two hundred years.

Benedict Arnold took a long look at the American-British conflict, and decided to be on the winning side.

That was his mistake.

Bibliography

Because much of my early research into Benedict Arnold's conspiracy was conducted with an idea to a dramatic film script, I did not behave in the orthodox scholarly fashion, but rather made notes of conversations and episodes which added historical veracity to the dramatic presentation. However, I did keep reference notes about sources, which I was able to re-consult when I realized that my research might turn into a book.

At every possible opportunity, I consulted original sources, but I admit freely to having consulted already printed volumes of letters and documents about Arnold, André, and their conspiracy. Perhaps the most rewarding of these is the publication of the Clinton Papers as an appendix to Carl Van Doren's *Secret History of the American Revolution* (1941). Another invaluable collection is Kenneth Roberts's editing of *March to Quebec: Journal of the Members of Arnold's Expedition* (1938). The two volumes of *The Spirit of Seventy-Six: The Story of the American Revolution as Told by the Participants*, by Henry Steele Commager and Richard B. Morris (1958), supplied lengthy quotations from letters and journals ordinarily excerpted or even truncated in other histories.

Another eyewitness account of the Revolution is provided by *Rebels and Redcoats*, by George F. Scheer and Hugh F. Rankin (1957). So also is *The Diary of the American Revolution*, by Frank Moore (1869), and currently available in a one-volume version edited by John Anthony Scott (1967).

While the events and personalities of history interest me the most, the outcome of battles is of supreme interest to an understanding of why things happened the way they did. I have an intellectual block to descriptions of military maneuvers (perhaps as a result of flunking ROTC in college), and battle-field movements have never been my strongest interest. But to tell the story of Benedict Arnold requires a rudimentary knowl-edge of how war was conducted in the eighteenth century. For this information I am indebted both to my colleague Wayne Daniels and to the two-volume *The War of the Ameri-can Revolution*, by Christopher Ward, edited by John Richard Alden (1952). This is, perhaps, the best introduction to the military aspects of the Revolution.

I must also acknowledge my deep debt to the efforts of three predecessors who have studied Benedict Arnold and his conspiracy. Even when I found myself in sharp disagreement with their conclusions, their scholarship was impeccable and their writings fired me with an enthusiasm for the subject. The first of these was Carl Van Doren, whose *Secret History of the American Revolution* is written moderately and without damning passion. The value of this book to future Arnold scholars, of course, is the inclusion of the Clinton Papers as an appendix.

Another biographer of Benedict Arnold, Willard M. Wal-lace, did his best in *Traitorous Hero* (1954) to understand the man, but he was writing about a traitor in an era when trea-son had turned America into a nation of neurotics. Wallace's book, published only two years after Julius and Ethel Rosen-berg were officially murdered by the United States govern-ment for a "crime" considerably less heinous than that of Benedict Arnold, suffers from the author's frequent editorializ-ing on Arnold's disgrace. Despite this, Wallace's book still re-mains one of the best biographies of Arnold.

Another book of the same era, James Thomas Flexner's *The Traitor and the Spy* (1953), is devoted equally to Arnold and André, with considerable attention to Peggy Shippen. Al-though not as doggedly as Wallace, Flexner seemed to feel the need to make periodic denunciations of the character of Ar-nold in light of his subsequent treason. However, both books are balanced biographies and should be read by any serious student of Benedict Arnold.

Whether either Wallace or Flexner would approach Bene-dict Arnold differently today, when the concepts of patriotism and treason have mellowed considerably, is academic. I do

know that when I started my own research, I definitely favored John André as opposed to Arnold. André seemed to be
the hero of the story, and the American general seemed tem-
peramental, egotistic, arrogant, and greedy; yet the more I
studied Arnold, the less apparent these flaws seemed. I con-
centrated on the original comments written by men who were
serving with him. Those who had known Arnold but wrote
about him after the treason often tried to vindicate themselves
by seeing who could be the most vituperative in his condemna-
tion of Arnold.

Other historians may dispute my conclusions, but until
we see all the documents pertaining to Washington, Arnold,
and the British in America, it is an academic discussion. Arnold, Peggy, and her Philadelphia family and friends burned
everything they could when his defection became known.
Perhaps they missed a few documents, the discovery of
which might require a fresh re-examination of the entire
affair.

Studying Benedict Arnold is much like studying Richard
III of England. The posthumous denunciations of both are
full of vilifications and slander. Yet an examination of the contemporary accounts written by their colleagues reveals that
both men were loved and respected as extraordinary leaders.
Anyone who wonders how the hated traitor Arnold could be
considered a hero need only consult Kenneth Roberts's excellent *March to Quebec*, a series of journals, diaries, and
letters by the men who marched with Arnold. Read the testi-
monials to Arnold's courage and popularity among the letters
and journals written before his defection. His men loved him
(a very few, of course, hated him). Every piece of writing to
come out of the American Revolution attests to the magnetism
and charm of the pre-treason Arnold.

So much has been written about Arnold that it is impossible to assemble a comprehensive bibliography. Rather, I
have tried to include those references which shed new or
original light on the man, along with those which are considered historically factual.

Abbatt, William. *The Crisis of the Revolution.* New York,
    1899. Obtainable now only in major libraries and oc-

casionally through rare-book dealers at exorbitant prices, this large book contains an antiquarian approach to the Arnold-André conspiracy, with photographs of many of the historical houses and landmarks which have since been destroyed. So few of the houses and sites now remain that Abbatt's book is a priceless collection of what André and Arnold saw during their eventful years.

Almon, John. *The Remembrancer.* 17 vols. London, 1775–84. This remarkable set of books, especially vol·me 5, contains the detailed accounts of such little-known affairs as the Baylor Massacre.

André, John. *Major Andre's Journal.* Tarrytown, 1930. This is the laconic memo book kept by the young André as aide-de-camp to General Grey during the Jersey campaign that includes the Paoli and Baylor massacres. (Arno Press, in conjunction with the New York *Times*, has recently republished this and many other similar books under the general series title of Eyewitness Accounts of the American Revolution.)

Burgoyne, John. *State of the Expedition from Canada.* London, 1780.

Fortescue, J. W. *A History of the British Army.* 14 vols. New York, 1899–1930.

Freeman, D. S. *George Washington.* 5 vols. New York, 1948–52.

Graham, J. *Life of General Daniel Morgan.* New York, 1856.

Green, F. V. *The Revolutionary War.* New York, 1911.

Irving, W. *Life of George Washington.* 5 vols. New York, 1956.

Lafayette. *Memoirs, Correspondence, and Manuscripts of General Lafayette.* 3 vols. London, 1837.

Lamb Papers. New-York Historical Society.

Leiby, A. C. *The Revolutionary War in the Hackensack Valley.* New Brunswick, N.J., 1962.

Mahan, A. T. *The Major Operations of the Navies in the War of American Independence.* Boston, 1913.

————. "The Naval Campaign of 1776 on Lake Champlain," in *Scribner's Magazine,* vol. 23 (1898).

Minutes of a Court of Inquiry upon the Case of Major John André. Albany, 1865.

Sargent, W. *Life and Career of Major André.* Boston, 1861.
For years this has been the definitive biography of André
and is chiefly responsible for the romantic legend that
hovers around him. Flexner's account of André in America has scrubbed off some of the saintly dust and describes
André with less emotion.

Thacher, J. *Military Journal of the American Revolution.*
Hartford, 1862.

van Schaack, H. C. *Life of Peter van Schaack.* New York,
1842.

Several miscellaneous articles, pamphlets, and other items
have aided me materially in this book. The detailed account
of the disinterment of Major André's bones in 1821 was described in *The Era* of December, 1901.

The story of André's reinterment in Westminster Abbey
near his monument is related in detail by Dean Arthur Penrhyn
Stanley in his fascinating *Historical Memorials of Westminster
Abbey* (2 vols.; New York, 1882). It was Dean Stanley who
persuaded Americans to erect a monument to André at the site
of his execution and first burial, and who himself prepared
the moving inscription for that monument.

For the specific facts of André's reinterment, I am indebted to N. H. MacMichael, F.S.A., Keeper of the Muniments (documents) at Westminster Abbey. Mr. MacMichael
expended considerable effort for what ultimately turned into
only a few sentences.

The account of the Baylor Massacre has been drawn from
a number of sources, chiefly the archeological findings of
Wayne M. Daniels, who supervised the discovery and disinterment of the bones of several members of Baylor's Dragoons
in 1967, and also from Dr. Griffiths' report to General Alexander after the doctor had personally interviewed the survivors
of the massacre, as reported in Almon's *Remembrancer.*

Index

Adams, John, 46
Adams, Samuel, 45
Alexander, Maj. Gen. William,
    89, 132, 226
Allen, Ethan, 4
André, John, 119
    early life, 120
    capture, 119
    release, 123
    Journal of, 126
    delivered to Continental
        Army, 211
    trial of, 227
    execution, 235
    memorial to, 245
    interment, 252
Arnold, Benedict
    early life, 34
    in New Haven, 36
    resignation of, 97
    "Dark Eagle," 106
    court-martial of, 159
    West Point letter, 181
    defection, 219
    departure for England, 241
    death, 246
Arnold, Benedict, Jr., 37
Arnold, Henry, 37

Arnold, Margaret Mansfield,
    37
    death, 47
Arnold, Richard, 37

Bache, Sarah Franklin, 152
Balcarres redoubt, 31, 114
Baylor, Col. George, 130
Baylor Massacre, 130
Baylor's Dragoons, 130
Bayonet, in military charges,
    30
Bemis Heights, 28, 108
Boles, Peter, 38
Boyd, Capt. Ebenezer, 207
Brandywine River, 127
Brant, Chief Joseph, 102
Breymann redoubt, 31, 114
Brown, Maj. John, 84, 95
Burgoyne, Gen. John, 27
Burr, Aaron, 52, 223
Buttonmould Bay (Button
    Bay), 78

Carleton, Sir Guy, 50
Catamount Tavern, 40
Chadd's Ford, 127
Chaudière River, 57

Charming Nancy, schooner, 156
Chew, Benjamin, 136
Clinton, Gen. Henry, 138
Clough, Maj. Alexander, 131
Colquehoun, Joseph, 197
Colquehoun, Samuel, 197
Commissions, purchase of, 123
Compo Point, 92
Concord, attack of, 39
Continental Congress, 45, 167
Cornwallis, Lord, 242
Cornwallis' surrender at York-town, 241
Cow Chace, The, 227
"Cowboys," 208
Cromwell, Oliver, 167
Crown Point, 45, 72

Dan Morgan's Virginians, 30
Danbury, sack and burning of, 93
De Blois, Elizabeth, 89
Dead River, 54
Deane, Silas, 47
Dearborn, Henry, 32, 109
Declaration of Independence, 72
Delaplace, Capt. William, 42
Dobbs Ferry, 192
Du Motier, Gilbert (Marquis de Lafayette), 145, 227

Easton, Col. James, 84
Egg Harbor, 157
Enos, Col. Roger, 56

Feltham, Lt. Jocelyn, 42
Fort Edward, 101, 102

Fort Griswold, 240
Fort Stanwix, siege of, 102
Fort Ticonderoga, 40, 97, 100
Fort Western (Fort Augusta), 54
Fortescue, Sir John, 33
Fortune, ship, 38
Franklin, Benjamin, 46
Franks, Maj. David, 155, 190
Fraser, Gen. Simon, 102
Freeman's Farm, 30, 110
French and Indian War, 34
French Revolution, 242

Gates, Maj. Gen. Horatio, 27, 81
Germain, Lord, 69, 122
Germantown, 129, 137
Great Carrying Place, the, 54
Green Mountain Boys, the, 40
Greene, Gen. Nathanael, 88, 226
Grey, Maj. Gen. Charles, 124
Griffiths, Dr. David, 132

Hackensack River, 128
Hamilton, Col. Alexander, 216
Hancock, John, 38
Hemlock sprigs, use of, 63
Hinman, Col. Benjamin, 46
Howe, Gen. William, 122

Jameson, Col. John, 211
Jefferson, Thomas, 46

Knox, Col. Henry, 119, 124
Knox, Mrs. Henry, 89
Kosciusko, Col. Thaddeus, 108

Lafayette, Gilbert du Motier, Marquis de, 145, 227
Lake Megantic, 57
Lamb, Col. John, 88, 191
Lathrop, Daniel, 34
Lathrop, Joseph, 34
Lee, Richard Henry, 90
Lexington, attack of, 39
Lincoln, Benjamin, 90
Livingston, Col. James, 197
Loring, Mrs. Joshua, 137

Mabie's Tavern, 226
McCrea, Jane, 103
McHenry, Maj. James, 221
Mahan, Adm. Alfred Thayer, 79
Massachusetts Committee of Public Safety, 40
Matlack, Joseph, 155
Mercenaries
  Brunswick, 28
  Hessian, 28, 107
"Meshianza," 144
Mifflin, Thomas, 90
Monk, Gen. George, 166
Montgomery, Brig. Gen. Richard, 49
  death, 66
Morgan, Dan, 34, 52
Muskets, use of, 30

Natanis, Chief, 54
New Bridge (River Edge), 131
Newburyport, 52
"No-Flint General," 132

Odell, Jonathan, 168

Ogden, Mathias, 52
Oswald, Eleazer, 52

Paoli, 128
Paulding, John, 209
Philadelphia, council of, 157
Phillips, Maj. Gen. William, 101
Pine's Bridge, 208
Plains of Abraham, 59
Point aux Trembles (Neuville), 61
Point Lévis, 58
Prevost, Mrs. Theodosia, 223

Quebec, storming of, 63

Reed, Joseph, 151
Richelieu River, 44
Robinson, Col. Beverley, 194

St. Clair, Arthur, 90, 102, 227
St. John's, 44, 60
St. Lawrence River, 49
St. Leger, Col. Burry, 102
Saratoga, battle of, 7, 111
Scammell, Col. Alexander, 226
Schuyler, Hon Yost, 104
Schuyler, Gen. Philip, 49, 81, 82
Senter, Dr. Isaac, 55
Sheldon, Col. Elisha, 192
Shewall, Robert, 157
Shippen, Peggy, 141
  marriage to Arnold, 154
  death, 246
Skenesboro (Whitehall, N.Y.), 70
"Skinners," 208

Smith, Joshua Hett, 193
Sneden's Landing, 193
Spencer, Gen. Joseph, 88
Stamp Act, 37
Stanley, Arthur Penrhyn, 252
Stansbury, Joseph, 162, 168
Stephen, Adam, 90
Steuben, Baron von, 227
Stony Point, 177
Sugar Act, 37
Sugar Loaf Hill, 100, 101

Talleyrand, Charles Maurice
    de, 243
Tallmadge, Maj. Benjamin,
    192
Tappan, 131
Tarleton, Col. Banastre, 124,
    129
Thompson, William, 52
"Traitor's Path, The," 218
Trenton, battle of, 87
Trumbull, Col. John, 87

Tryon, Gov. William, 92

Valcour Island, 72
Valley Forge, 145
Van Wart, Isaac, 209
Varick, Lt. Col. Richard, 109
Verplanck's Landing, 177
Virginians, Dan Morgan's, 30
Von Knyphausen, Gen. Wil-
    helm, 127

War of 1812, 248
Washington, Gen. George
    disciplinary methods, 81
    meeting with Arnold, 47
    retreat from Manhattan, 85
Waterbury, Gen. David, 70
Wayne, Gen. Anthony, 101,
    124, 226
Webb, Col. Samuel, 209
Wilkinson, Col. James, 110
Williams, David, 209
Wooster, Gen. David, 67

THE AUTHOR

BRIAN RICHARD BOYLAN was born in Chicago
and attended Loyola University. In addition
to being the author of ten fiction and non-
fiction books, he has had wide experience as a
professional director in all media, and he is
currently working on two off-Broadway pro-
ductions. He is married, has three children, and
lives in Hillsdale, New Jersey.